Feminist Pilgrimage

Also by Stacy Russo

Nonfiction
- *A Better World Starts Here: Activists and Their Work* (Sanctuary Publishers)
- *Love Activism* (Litwin Books)
- *We Were Going to Change the World: Interviews with Women from the 1970s and 1980s Southern California Punk Rock Scene* (Santa Monica Press)
- *The Library as Place in California* (McFarland)

Edited Collections
- *Life as Activism: June Jordan's Writings from the Progressive* (Litwin Books)

Poetry
- *Everyday Magic* (Finishing Line Press)
- *The Moon and Other Poems* (Dancing Girl Press)

Feminist Pilgrimage
Journeys of Discovery

Edited by *Stacy Russo*

Litwin Books
Sacramento, CA

Published in 2020 by Litwin Books.

Litwin Books
PO Box 188784
Sacramento, CA 95818

http://litwinbooks.com/

This book is printed on acid-free paper.

Library of Congress Cataloging-in-Publication Data

Names: Russo, Stacy Shotsberger, 1970- author.
Title: Feminist pilgrimage : journeys of discovery / Stacy Russo.
Description: Sacramento : Litwin Books, 2020. | Summary: "A collection of
    personal essays by contemporary feminist educators, scholars, artists,
    and writers, imagining the concept of "pilgrimage" in their lives
    through a diverse exploration"-- Provided by publisher.
Identifiers: LCCN 2020028154 | ISBN 9781634001113 (paperback)
Subjects: LCSH: Women in public life--United States. | Women--United
    States--History. | Feminism--United States--History.
Classification: LCC HQ1391.U5 R87 2020 | DDC 305.40973--dc23
LC record available at https://lccn.loc.gov/2020028154

Contents

The contributors to this collection voted to award royalties from sales to the Women's Center for Creative Work (WCCW) in Los Angeles, California. The WCCW cultivates feminist creative communities and practices with a feminism that prioritizes women of color, queer, trans and nonbinary folx, and other marginalized communities. The WCCW houses the main branch of the Feminist Library on Wheels, offers workshops, provides artist grants, and performs various other important work to build community.

Introduction

The pilgrimage narrative is one found throughout literary history with *The Canterbury Tales* being an early example. Homer's *Odyssey*, although arguably more of a wandering, may also be considered an early pilgrim's tale. Contemporary literature is abundant with pilgrimage-style narratives, including many popular memoirs, such as Cheryl Strayed's *Wild: From Lost to Found on the Pacific Crest Trail*.[1] As a journey, a pilgrimage is similar to a quest. Something, often wisdom or self-discovery of the spiritual or internal nature, is to be found and brought home. Going on a pilgrimage invites discovery. It is frequently steeped in the magic of adventure, the unknown landscape, openness, and uncharted territory. A pilgrimage requires courage and an embrace of uncertainty. The brave pilgrim welcomes change.

Feminist pilgrimages carry all the wonder and discovery of the classical variety, but there is something markedly and wonderfully different when a journey is taken through a feminist lens. The personal essays in this collection, written by contemporary feminist educators, writers, scholars, and artists, go deep and examine one's engagement with the world on a path of liberation, struggle, self-determination, and often radical self-love. It was through my own pilgrimage experiences that the idea of this beautiful project came to be.

When I left a troubled marriage nearly ten years ago now, I found myself quickly planning adventures. In my new and peaceful apartment I posted a list titled "Places to Visit and Other Possibilities." It was through

---

1   Cheryl Strayed, *Wild: From Lost to Found on the Pacific Crest Trail* (New York, NY: Knopf, 2012).

my many travels that some of my deepest healing occurred. What did I do? I flew into Bozeman, Montana, and stayed several nights at a wolf sanctuary before driving to Wyoming and South Dakota. I spent several luminous days in Taos, New Mexico, including one day where I decided to drive across the state line into Colorado. I got out of my car on an empty and silent Colorado road with snow-topped mountains around, raised my arms up, and let out several loud cheers in celebration of being alive and free. I flew to Seattle and drove back down through Portland, and onto San Francisco with the beautiful Oregon and California coast at my side. I traveled to Brooklyn, specifically to spend time with the artist Judy Chicago's *The Dinner Party* that is now permanently housed at the Brooklyn Museum (see Cindy Rinne's essay in this collection for an earlier pilgrimage to view *The Dinner Party*). I also returned to Berkeley several times, picking up my annual ritual walk that I chose to write about for this collection. During these walks I became stronger while reconnecting with my younger undergraduate self who would have never imagined domestic abuse was in her future. These journeys liberated me. Traveling solo, I regained my courage. I built my resilience.

While thinking of my journeys one day, the seed for this project was planted. Knowing the diversity and magic that often comes from collaborative gatherings, I wondered about other feminists' pilgrimages. This led to me putting out a call for proposals to see if there would be an interest from others in participating (the original call is provided at the end of this volume). Not only did I receive several dozen proposals, but I was overwhelmed with what arrived to my in-box. The proposals were stunningly good, making the selection process difficult. I also quickly discovered that there were many ways to imagine a pilgrimage.

Opening up the call to a broad audience with diverse experiences and voices brought perspectives that allowed me to consider alternative visions. In my mind, initially, the concept of pilgrimage involved literal, definitely not figurative, travel and I realized my vision often mirrored my experiences as a solo traveler. Although some of the proposals fit this vision I had, I was surprised by the proposals and found myself opening to other ideas I never imagined. Perhaps one of the most unique proposals came from Trysh Travis, whose pilgrimage is a mental one as she returns to try and make sense of uncertain occurrences that took place many years ago during a high school afternoon. I invite you to be pulled in by her "On Bluebird Trail" that appears here. I was also intrigued by Amanda LaTasha

Armstrong's understanding of her Black feminist journey in academia as a pilgrimage. Please travel along with Armstrong in "I Didn't Expect This!: How Healing and Care Became a Part of My Black Feminist Journey in Academia." While reading a proposal by the Lazy Bottom Retreat members, I felt wonderfully envious and inspired by the nine women who created a biannual group pilgrimage for themselves. I encourage you to read their collaborative piece "Lazy Bottom Retreats: Where No One is Actually Lazy or a Bottom."

This collection demonstrates how creative feminist thinking is. It also illustrates the deep understanding and connection the contributors have to the concept of pilgrimage. I welcome you to join them on their adventures.

Stacy Russo
Santa Ana, California
November 2019

Blow

Lise Weil

Each of us is so much more than we think we are... We are air exhaled by hemlocks, we are water plowed by whales, we are matter born in stars, we are children of deep time.

Great Tide Rising, Kathleen Dean Moore[1]

It was our last day in Baja. I had come here to spend time with whales. I am not fond of heat and Baja is *hot*. And truthfully, whales, though I worshipped them from afar, had not been my favourite mammals. Despair drove me to Baja. It was March 2017 and I was still reeling from the elections and what they said about the U.S. and our chances of redeeming ourselves as a species. Could nature recover from our relentless assaults? Was there any reason to hope? I thought the whales might have some wisdom to offer. That I would be travelling with a women's wilderness outfit and a guide who communicated with whales seemed to increase the likelihood of this outcome.

When a blue whale first approached—we were camped on the shore of the Sea of Cortez, just gathering for our morning circle—all the other women fell to their knees and stayed there as we watched her circle the bay

---

1   Kathleen Dean Moore, *Great Tide Rising: Towards Clarity and Moral Courage in a Time of Planetary Change* (Berkeley, CA: Counterpoint, 2016), 79–80.

(a mama and her calf our guide told us). In circle, the women spoke in tones of reverence and rapture. I abstained. I had seen those huge bodies blowing and breaching and yes it was impressive, they were BIG (the biggest mammals on the face of the earth, we had been informed, up to two city blocks in length), and these enormous creatures had come to us, or so the others insisted, come repeatedly, but I felt nothing.... certainly by contrast with my companions. Or, to be honest, I felt rage. What the fuck makes you think they are coming for us? Why the fuck would they want to come to us? After what we've done to them? Done to the oceans. I said this one night around the campfire, my face wet with tears which in all honesty were probably less tears of shame for our species than pain at not being able to feel what the others felt, at feeling separate from them.

But after five days on the Sea of Cortez, spying one fluke after another, watching those giant bodies dive and surface and dive again, I had come to believe, I can't say how exactly, that maybe yes they did love us and yes they had come for us. Now we were staying in cabins on San Ignacio Bay on the other side of the peninsula. San Ignacio is a protected lagoon where gray whales come to calve and where for this reason they were murdered *en masse* by humans in the nineteenth and for much of the twentieth century. But in 1977, a fisherman in the bay received a visit from a mama gray and her calf who would not leave the side of his boat until he had stroked the baby. Since then, San Ignacio has become a pilgrimage site, a place where humans can venture out in boats and be pretty sure that they'll not only see but be able to touch a gray whale. It was now our fourth day here on the lagoon and already its rippling waters had come to feel like one of those neighborhoods that was sacred to me because *she* lived there—the woman I loved— and any second she might suddenly appear.

It had been a hard morning. The hardest of the trip. Several days earlier, after a rough day of paddling that had done me in, I had leapt to the aid of someone who was heaving a double kayak out of the water—in the spirit of pitching in but also so as not to be outdone by my younger travel mates. In the process I pulled something skeletal badly out of whack. It had caught up to me the day before and I had barely slept. All night I had dreamt of a chiropractor—could I find one in this area? In the morning in the circle I told the dream and then, since the dream seemed to be wanting it of me, asked if anyone in the circle knew anything about alignment. There were on this trip an assortment of healers and yoga teachers and I was secretly hoping someone might offer to help straighten me out. No one did. I felt—there is only one word for it—rejected. No one wanted to take on my case, my crooked, aging body. An old haunted place—not beautiful enough—I went back to it.

But there is something I've left out here, something about that sleepless night that feels important to say. I have spent many nights lying awake with one kind of ailment or another just listening to the minutes tick away. This night was not like any of those. Because throughout the hours, and the muscular cramps that seized my neck and held it in a vice, I remained completely calm. I remained calm because I had every confidence I would be healed....in fact it occurred to me during that long night that there is no healing without affliction. So maybe affliction is necessary? I was afflicted, and I needed this affliction so that I could be healed.

I had been reading about whales the night before, suddenly ravenous for knowledge about these beings about whom until now my main source of information had been *Moby Dick*. In one book I read that just by the way they navigate, conducting waves of light and sound, whales serve to bring everything into balance. "Planetary alignment" is how the writer put it. Well if they could align planets why not one human body?

In late morning, after the circle, we went out in the boats. The driver of my boat was Sextos, a big burly Mexican who never ventured out into the lagoon without his flute. "A blow!" someone would shout, pointing, and all binoculars would take aim as Sextos sped up to get near, then cut the motor. Soon he would unfurl the bandanna in which he'd wrapped his flute, pick it up, and begin playing. The whales would arrive within minutes. One time what looked like a whole pod came and stirred the waters beside our boat, rolling over and spyhopping and cavorting while we raced from side to side of the boat in anticipation. At some point we knew at least one of them would sidle up to us.

I can still feel it, seeing one of those huge mottled gray bodies arcing and diving and arcing again until she was just alongside the boat, how alive it would get down in my belly. As if at one time that gray mottled body had been in mine. As if it had *been* mine? In these moments there is only body, there is just you and your friends on this boat and beside you now practically rubbing up against the gunwales, this giant gray slippery body of the "baby" who is the biggest animal you have ever touched. There is only the feel of the slick rubbery skin against your hand as the body moves up and down, the feel of your hand inside the baby's mouth when you manage to push past the soft fringe of the baleen and he seems to grip onto it, the feel of that rubbery skin against your lips the one time you manage to attach your mouth to it—"*Bésame! Bésame!*" Sextos is yelling, kiss them, they love it!

A Somali friend of mine told me that the most horrible moment of her childhood—and she lived through mass killings—was the first time she looked at herself in a mirror. She was five or six years old. It was not that she did not like what she saw. It was that until that moment she had lived in the world as a purely sentient being. Now, she said, all was *localized* perception. Then, it was her whole body that perceived and the world was completely alive. *Whole-body perception.* Here, with the whales, I had an inkling of what she was talking about.

This is all there is in the world, just these human bodies around you these animal bodies in the water and the body of the ocean and you, who are suddenly both heavier and lighter than you've ever been, have been given the ballast you have always needed, yet are floating in watery ether. This is what it is to know a being so big, so massive in its primal ISness, that its waves ripple out to the far edges of the world and leave no being untouched.

When the boat pulls in to shore Sextos helps us disembark then gathers us all in a circle and has us dance sideways together and then blow kisses at each other. "Love is in the air," he sings. It *is*, I can feel it, we have been loved by the whales and now we all love each other, we can't help it! And there is not a crooked bone or aching muscle in my body.

But the whales are not done with me yet. Or I am not done with them. I am going out one more time in the afternoon. My last chance. As the boat pulls out I wonder if I'm being greedy. There are only five of us from the trip, wanting to get in our last hellos, and our driver is a woman who is mostly quiet as we head out to sea. The water is rough now, rougher than it's been before, it is harder to spy the whales and for a long time we don't see any. I notice myself beginning to long…. to hanker. To crave. Please whales just one last time. As if I haven't already had enough. As if they haven't already given me…. EVERYTHING! Oh but this is my last day, my last chance. Please mama please baby, just one last time. But haven't they been teaching me patience? Being one with what is, whatever that is?? Isn't that their palpable wisdom?? Obviously I have not taken it in as I watch myself getting more and more anxious…..Only twenty minutes left and still we have not spied one whale. Until, at last, yes!!! Just fifty feet from our boat, a mama and her large calf, frolicking, seeming to want our company.

And now the baby is right up against the boat and the others are all rushing to one side to stroke him—no doubt jonesing like me. Most of them manage to get their hands on him, but he shoots off before I can in-sinuate myself. Damn! But now... a giant body moving towards us. The mama? Yes! Just feet away!! This I will not miss, we have been sending the mothers our love now for days, we can't help feeling the most aching grat-itude to them for the way they keep offering up their young. And now... now I get to thank her with my hands!! I push my way in and extend myself far over the side of the boat. Oh Mama come come you're the best mama we love you so much....She is now so close just a few more inches and my fingers will make contact.... Instead !!!! Sudden shock of spray. Wet salt spray jet spray and now WET hair WET jacket WET pants and even the boat WET now filling with water and your friends and the driver also wet and pointing at you, laughing—you who all week have been trying to pro-tect your hair from the salt water!! You, who, when the shock relents, are laughing the purest loudest most HEARTY laughter of your entire life. Also the longest, as it goes on and on and on... because this great mama has just sprayed you, has chosen this moment of your readiness your open-ness to blow on you with all the force of her giant lungs. There is NOTH-ING now but this and then for hours there is only this... complete aban-don to this moment, of laughter.... And love.

This past week on the news there have been reports about those be-loved gray whales washing up on California beaches dead or dying of mal-nourishment. The condition of the blue whales I'm told is also deteriorat-ing, due to climate change. This news is or should be sad beyond measure for us humans. For one who has come to recognize whales as her teachers, it is devastating.

I've been a feminist editor and activist for most of my adult life. In addition to battling patriarchy, operating out of a feminist consciousness for me has meant—my early guides here were lesbian visionaries like Au-dre Lorde, Susan Griffin, and Mary Daly—cultivating joy and wholeness of being. What I learned in Baja was that this mission can only be fully ac-complished once we enlist the participation of the nonhuman world. If it feels imperative to me at this moment in time that feminist vision encom-pass more than the social body, that it also be about animal bodies and the body of the earth, this is not only because the fate of these other bodies is so precarious right now. Even more, it is because without those other bod-ies, without being able to feel them as part of us, we are so much smaller, so much less powerful, so much less capable of love, and laughter and joy.

Peregrina

LeeRay M. Costa

As you enter the cathedral at Santiago, may you be blessed with the
foolishness to think that you can make a difference in the world, so that when
you return home, you will do the thing which others tell you cannot be done.

A pilgrim blessing

People ask me when I decided to walk 400 miles on the Camino de Santiago, also known as the Way of St. James, but honestly I can't remember. My pilgrimage was at least ten years in the planning before the inaugural stamp was inked into my pilgrim passport and I found my first painted yellow way marker at the base of Sé Cathedral. The impulse to complete this pilgrimage felt essential to my being; you might say that I had long been on the path that led me to Portugal—the land of my ancestors—and eventually to Santiago de Compostela.

There were numerous reasons for my pilgrimage: personal, professional, physical, and spiritual, and it was a gift to have these varied aspects of my life converge on the path. A university sabbatical allowed me the time to go on pilgrimage in the first place, and my work on feminist contemplative pedagogies and spiritual activism provided a professional rationale for what was otherwise a deeply personal and spiritual adventure. At forty-eight years old, I was at a critical mid-way point in my career as a professor of Gender and Women's Studies and in search of ways to be more authentic in my work and in my life. Going on pilgrimage promised a break from the everyday, and offered a sacred, liminal space in which to reflect, explore, and be open to possibility with each and every breath. Journeying as a *peregrina*[1] offered up a different sort of relationship to time and space, to nature, to other people, and to my very being in the world.

There is a certain irony in that pilgrimage, a largely solitary act, taught me precious lessons about the importance of relationality. Though I was joined on my journey by my dear friend and pilgrim-sister Annemarie, much of our time walking—together and apart—was in silence. I chose the Portuguese route specifically because of my own family history, and pictured myself walking in the footsteps of my Portuguese ancestors, on paths traversed by thousands before me. Prior to embarking on my thirty-three-day journey I visualized these ancestors whispering in my ear, walking by my side, encouraging me to go on.

These connections, though at first only imagined, materialized on the third day as I came upon a graveyard in the outskirts of Azambuja. Climbing the stone steps and entering the sacred grounds, I was struck by how alive the graveyard felt. Carefully tended by the living, graves were adorned with fresh flowers and small gifts, and their headstones displayed photos of the deceased. Initially I held back as I observed a woman carry a pitcher of water to a grave, lovingly clean it, and then gently bestow a kiss. I was profoundly moved by witnessing what felt like a holy act. As I slowly navigated my way among the marble markers, I read the carved names to myself; Vieira, Borges, Pico, Perriera, Madeiros, Citra, Costa. These were my family names— my name—laid out before me. A wave of sorrow pulsed through my body, reducing me to sobs. I felt intimately rooted to the people and the land in ways I could not explain, but felt deep in my bones.

The Portuguese have a word to describe this deep emotional state of nostalgia, melancholic longing, or missing-ness: *saudade*. Writing in 1912, the Portuguese poet Teixeira de Pascoaes defined saudade as "desire for the beloved thing, made painful by its absence."[2] Saudade is the constant presence of absence, and "the word's morbid poetics throw light on how

---

1 Peregrina is the feminine form of pilgrim in Portuguese.

2 Michael Amoruso, "Saudade: The Untranslatable Word for the Presence of Absence," *Aeon*, October 8, 2018, https://aeon.co/ideas/saudade-the-untranslateable-word-for-the-presence-of-absence.

affective ties make for a meaningful human life."[3] The concept of saudade provided me with a culturally relevant and specific framework for making sense of what I was feeling and experiencing, both materially and spiritually, and offered up a new entry point into my feminist social justice work.

The experience in the graveyard took me by surprise, but perhaps I had ignored the portents. By the second day I had already sensed that my father, who had transitioned beyond this life twelve years earlier, was accompanying me on the camino. Having grown up in Hawai'i, he had never had the opportunity to travel to Portugal. I was confident that if he was still alive, he'd be following my path by car, meeting me at the end of each day for a hearty and flavorful meal and bottomless glasses of homemade Portuguese wine as we regaled each other with our adventures.

My father made his presence known in the wispy, silver-green *funcho* that grew everywhere in the river plain of the country. During my childhood visits with him in Hawai'i, he had indefatigably pointed out the fennel plant to me, saying "Funcho! Look at the funcho LeeRay!" He'd snap off a few strands, rub them between his dry, rough hands and while closing his eyes, inhale deeply. Grinning he'd offer the fragrant broken fronds to my nose as if planting deep into my senses a seed, preparing me for this future harvest of reconnection. As I walked, funcho became a welcome, reassuring companion on the journey, and I marveled at my newfound herb relative.

Though only parts of the route meandered through forests, fields, and green spaces, and along beaches, rivers, and marshes, I found myself at first pondering and then fully experiencing my intimate relationship with the natural world. I took note of every living being that crossed my path—lizards, rabbits, snakes, and insects—and wrote about them in my journal. I learned to recognize and name the flowers, trees, and plants, and to honor their presence. As we ritually greeted one another each morning and throughout the day, they became familiar, trusted companions and it became increasingly difficult, even ridiculous to think of them as separate from me. While intellectually I had long understood the concept of interconnectedness, it was my daily encounter with the physical and natural world that allowed it to become embodied knowledge.

This interconnectedness encompassed the bodies of complete strangers with whom I had both fleeting and sustained encounters. These camino

---

3   Amoruso, "Saudade."

angels emerged again and again on my journey, their gifts as varied as cherries, water, bandages, beds, kind words, and tender caresses. I lost count of the times that elderly Portuguese women touched me, as if to both nurture and bolster me for the journey ahead. Antonio, a lovely man who opened up his closed café just for me and my companion to take a boots-off break, read us his poetry while his wife prepared food and coffee for us. When he caught sight of my naked blistered and bandaged feet, he clutched his heart with his hand and squeezed my shoulder, verklempt with admiration for my physical sacrifice. He had never made the journey to Santiago himself, yet his café was a literal shrine to pilgrims from around the world whose small trinkets, notes, and postcards were prominently displayed.

I experienced the kindness of strangers so often on my journey that gratitude overwhelmed me and it became impossible not to see the divine spirit in each person. In Santa Clara, a suburb bordering Coimbra, I paused outside a gated home to wait in the shade for my companion to catch up. I observed an elderly couple in their eighties in the process of saying farewell to their children and grandchildren, waving as the car pulled away. Noticing me, the grandmother approached to ask if I was a peregrina, and was eventually joined by her husband. After endeavoring to communicate in four separate languages including that of the heart, the couple invited us into their courtyard to share some homemade wine. We laughed as the grandfather insisted that he fill our water bottles with his private vintage to fortify us for the journey. Sending us on our way with good humor and warm hugs, they asked us to remember them and to pray for them in Santiago. These generous gifts were a persistent intervention into the taken for granted cynicism I had absorbed in the academy and the social, racial, and economic divisions that negatively structure my everyday life in the United States.

Encountering these beautiful souls challenged my pessimistic assumptions and forced me to admit my own hubris. During one of our café stops, my companion and I observed another pilgrim, a middle-aged white man with a large pack and wooden walking stick. Immediately we speculated about who he was and what he was about. I feel ashamed now to think of how I brazenly pre-judged this absolute stranger. Days later, he was wordlessly and tenderly bandaging my blistered, aching feet with silk tape he had brought from the Netherlands. Being vulnerable with this stranger that I had dismissed without knowing, was humbling and heart-opening. Teaching me love and humility with his simple act of service and care, this pilgrim would have a profound effect on the way I relate to others, and on how I understand and teach feminism as a way of connection across difference.

Each day as I got closer to Santiago, my camino family of pilgrims took shape. What a joy it was to enter into a new town, hot, sweaty and tired, and have friendly faces waiting, calling my name. I was the prodigal daughter returning home, being received with love again and again and again. Being embraced into this community without expectation or judgement was a welcome reprieve especially on days that were physically and/or emotionally taxing. Fellow pilgrims were rarely interested in what you had accomplished or produced, your education, title, income, or identity. Rather, they queried: *Where did you walk from today? Have you eaten? How are your feet? What do you need? And the deeper question on everyone's minds: What brought you to the camino?* Pilgrim conversations were often more honest and more profound than social exchanges back home. Though each pilgrim walked for unique and private reasons, there was a shared vulnerability and devotion in simply being there in the first place, and thus a feeling of human connection and affection. While there was certainly risk involved in sharing with others the pain and persistent questioning each of us carried in addition to our backpacks, it was perhaps not as meaningful or as illuminating as risking confrontation with ourselves.

Ambling through aromatic eucalyptus forests, planted by the Portuguese to sell as paper pulp, I was captivated by their delicate peeling bark. Touching their paper-thin curling skins and tender exposed trunk, I pondered my own shedding and new growth. The trees surrendering their skins metaphorically echoed the image of my naked body that kept reappearing in my vivid and nightly dreams during the first few weeks of the journey. In the baring of skin and soul, I learned how to release beliefs, expectations, and socialized ways of being that had limited me personally, and hindered my chosen work as a feminist teacher and social justice advocate. Step by step, tear by tear, and laugh by laugh, I charted a path toward purpose, wholeness, and interconnection in a context where these qualities and forms of intelligence are not always valued.

The gift of pilgrimage is that self-reflection is unavoidable when one is alone with one's thoughts and feelings. Walking in silence up to eight hours each day, whether along ancient cobblestone roads, on windswept beach boardwalks, or even underneath twenty-first century highway overpasses, provides ample opportunity for developing self-awareness and self-observation. This attention to self can be simultaneously invigorating and excruciatingly painful as we confront our entitlements, failures, and human imperfections, both as individuals and as members of complex communities.

I recall the day I finally made it to the section of the journey named Camino de Costa. This, I thought, is the heart of my camino, named as it is for my Portuguese lineage. I had romanticized and fantasized about what walking this section of the journey along the sea would feel like. Surely it would be delightful and full of ease, and I would luxuriate in the ocean breezes and briny air as I recalled my childhood home in Hawai'i. Instead it proved to be the most challenging and distressing day of my pilgrimage. Pummeled by gale force winds and the relentless needling of my skin by innumerable grains of sand amassed at this very location over centuries, my body struggled to make way. Shoulders hunched forward, my body folded in on itself and I fought to maintain control of my poles. Without their grounding support, I feared the wind would literally sweep me up and away, lost, like the stories of my ancestors. This carried on for hours as the clouds collected above and the blue sky succumbed to slate grey. I wept streams of salty tears as I pushed on, overcome by doubt and fear, berating myself for taking on this foolish task. Why? Why did I choose this path? What was I thinking? Eventually I made it to a place of shelter, and out of nowhere appeared one of my fellow camino pilgrims who had become like family, a welcome surprise and a reminder that challenge is always punctuated with joy and that the things we believe in demand endurance and are worth fighting for – including ourselves. It would take months for me to fully process my experience that day and its revelations.

This experience, like countless others during my pilgrimage, offered the opportunity for discovering my own human-made limitations, for imagining how to be otherwise, and for learning humility. Self-reflection gives us insight into the why and how of our lives, and reminds us to be compassionate, both with ourselves and in our interactions with others. This is the way of kindness as well as accountability, and the requisite path toward collective freedom.

Pilgrimaging for me was a form of meditation in motion that provided a sensation of spaciousness that was absent from my hectic, overscheduled everyday life as a working mother, partner, daughter, and community member. Beyond creating room for self-reflection, walking the camino offered an invitation to spirit to reveal itself, affirming yet another form of relationality. Or perhaps more accurately, spirit was always already present, and I just had to practice being quiet enough, attentive enough, and open enough to recognize it and welcome it in with curiosity, humility, and love. In the secular world of higher education, spirit is suspect, often seen as an atavistic reminder of a pre-modern, unscientific, and retrograde past. This was a lesson I learned early as an undergraduate student while writing an honors thesis that explored whether sociologists could also be believers and practitioners in the spiritual communities that they researched. In the years that followed I endeavored to suppress this part of my own human knowing and being in the world, only to have it tenaciously and resolutely reassert itself as I approached middle age. The solitude and spaciousness of walking the camino provided just the right conditions, not only for upending this dispiriting framework but also for cracking open my heart and soul, releasing notions of I-me-ness and remembering the we-ness that is our divine inheritance. Even that description feels wholly inadequate, superficial, and trite. As Jungian analyst and author James Hollis writes, "When one has had an authentic engagement with mystery, it is neither definable nor explicable nor transmittable to others."[4]

Rather than try to explain or define the ineffable, I will conclude by telling you what pilgrimaging in the land of my ancestors has meant to me and the work I have chosen to do in this lifetime. Walking the camino has been (and continues to be) a journey of self-exploration, relational learning, and communal healing. The personal and professional healing I experienced during my pilgrimage was not mine alone, but energetically reverberated through space and time to heal both my ancestors and my future descendants, and the lives of those each one of us has touched. It is a healing embodied in daily encounters with self, ancestors, strangers, nature, and spirit, and in the knowing that we belong to one another, and must fight for one another's wholeness—not just when it is easy, but especially when it is hard and painful and we think we may fail. Because my joy is your joy, and your suffering is my suffering. It is a healing that I have carried back to my adopted home of Virginia, into my personal relationships, into the classroom in my work as a college teacher, and into my daily conversations about what it means to live a feminist life in the United States at this historical moment.

---

4   James Hollis, *Finding Meaning in the Second Half of Life* (New York, NY: Gotham Books, 2005), 174.

Spanish poet Antonio Machado has written that there is no way, but that the pilgrim makes the way as she walks.[5] As I continue on my pilgrimage—informed by my ancestors and the feminist and social justice activists I hold dear—these mantras give voice to my intentions and guide my way:

May I live and work with spirit.
May I be a builder of bridges.
May I make meaningful connections across difference.
May I listen attentively.
May I love fully.
And may I inspire others to walk the path of justice.

Note

With deepest gratitude to: Annemarie Carroll, my pilgrim-sister—for sharing the journey; Karen Cardozo and Darla Schumm, trusted friends—for collegiality, honest feedback, and encouragement; Luke Vilelle, librarian extraordinaire—for providing writing space and support; and Hollins University for financially supporting my sabbatical that made this pilgrimage possible.

---

5 Antonio Machado, *Campos de Castilla (Fields of Castille)*, trans. Stanley Appelbaum (Mineola, NY: Dover Publications, 2007/1912). [I have paraphrased here and replaced "he" with "she."]

A Pilgrimage... Atonement

Indra Chopra

Be not afraid of life. Believe that life is worth living, and your belief will help create the fact.

William James[1]

December 2017: I feel my body, one tentative palm followed by another; my limbs appear straight, not knotted. But, wait. Why is my heart thumping? A drum roll to alert organs to perform.

The rawness in the chest, a cracked open walnut.... a groan. "She is awake." "Would you like a drink?" "Coca Cola." The doctor agrees and I am allowed a sip of the soda. I focus on the "scrub" face and wonder at his identity. The nurse clues me in to the harrowing CABG procedure (open heart surgery) lasting more than six hours, the vigil in the Intensive Care Unit, and the new me with working arteries and a pig or porcine valve.

I am not surprised as matters of the heart are a genealogical condition handed down from my paternal grandfather to father, uncles, and four brothers. So how could I, daughter, be spared? Actually, I was hoping I would be, by mother's genes, but no such luck.

---

1   William James, *The Will to Believe: And Other Essays on Popular Philosophy* (London: Longmans Green and Co, 1897/1907), 62.

If only I could do away with the pain. Images catch up, juxtapose into each other. In the next dream sequence from my hospital bed I am a Bedouin kid playing in a tent with diaphanous sheets flailing in the hot desert breeze, camels squatting nearby and there was father in a *thawb* (Arab dress) standing in front of the Sphinx. I have never visited Egypt, but father had, or maybe my new blood coursing through my body had, courtesy of some Afghan donor, and it transported me to Arabia. (The Delhi hospital requires patients' kin to supplement the blood bank for the used blood and there are many patients from neighboring countries).

I toss and turn searching for the one image constant in my dreams. Images of mother (she passed away in February 2000) in different avatars: the Lady in French Chiffon saris, crimson lipped, diamond and pearl jewelry, red stilettos; the bleary eyed widow in white breaking her glass bangles (Hindu tradition insisted widows eschew worldly embellishments. It is changing now.); the cajoling, entreating, scolding custodian; the struggling body trying to overcome multiple health issues.

We troubled her, four boys and me, and she did not blink. We never paused to ask if this was what she had envisioned for herself when she left graduate studies midway to marry my father, her parents' choice. A perfect foil for her ambitious husband who wanted an English speaking wife to entertain his Anglophile friends, to manage a "bungalow" purchased from a departing Englishman, and to educate children in English-medium convent schools. (In the 1940s the British were still in India.) It was a never-ending list and she ticked it with élan.

Images oscillate… Shiny button eyes squint through strands of curly hair, pitter-patter of feet echoing in the gloomy narrow passage connecting the living and dining areas of our house, arms flailing in all directions…. "No mummy, I do not want to drink milk."

"But you must." The nurse is insisting as I am propped up for my medicines. The pain is excruciating. An earlier time I would have wriggled past to hide in my own *mihrab* (favorite spot).

The nurse morphs into mother and the thick white cotton curtains into colorful wooden blinds blocking the summer sun in our patio. I focus on the tableaux. Ultimately mother gives up and I run past her out into the courtyard and on to the steps leading to the terrace to my safe haven, my refuge for plotting/sulking against four brothers and her.

Sometimes birds gave me company, especially the koel, ever ready for a song duel till it flew away in search of an unsuspecting crow's nest to lay her eggs. I never saw the bird and would follow the sound as she/he hopped from tree to tree. The koel was my night light; my search-song as there was no Amazon Alexa then. Years later, whenever and wherever (Delhi, Hong Kong), the 'koo-oo' symbolized the romanticism of courage to me. It was recently that I saw the koel with its black glossy skin and discovered it is the male of the species who 'koo-oos' during the monsoon/mating season.

The koel appearance coincided with the mango season, from March till June, and for us the beginning of adventures. There were seven mango trees, a jackfruit tree, guavas, custard apple, and other fruit trees in our compound. Our gardener, who slept under the shade of the mango trees during the day, was the human CCTV camera, a hawk-eyed vigilante for neighborhood kids. He would let us, me and two younger brothers, climb the trees to pluck raw mangoes. I pestered him for a few extra and he gave in to my demands. He knew I saw him collect fruits, nibbled by parrots and squirrels, plus a few fresh ones, to take home and he was worried that I would snitch on him.

It was an idyllic life growing up amidst nature with the fresh morning breeze from the three holy rivers, Ganga, Yamuna, and mythical Saraswati, the 'Sangam troika' of Hindu mythology. Every day at 4 a.m., during summer vacations, we would be on the riverbank waiting for the hired boat. The slithering cool sands between our toes, hymns reverberating through the air.... instant *moksha* or a state of transcendence, what *sadhus* (religious men in orange robes) preached about. Evenings were boat rides with visiting relatives to watch the sun dive in for its holy dip and disappearance in the waters.

Ouch!!! A jab and I was on a hospital bed. I must have been crying out for mother as the excruciating pain seared through my chest. The nurse smiled, an angelic smile to soothe my nerves, a mutilated me wrapped up in tubes, lying helpless.

As an atheist I did not want to fault my 'karma' for making me go through this pain. But maybe my life cannot be pinned down to a single word or incident and needed to be told in dazzling fragments, shards, jigsaw pieces and reflected images.

I am at Stanford University for a 1975 summer course in journalism, watching Orson Welles' *Citizen Kane* to review for an assignment. But it is a newsreel of never-ending summer delights, of sorrows and losses difficult to erase, the punches of goodwill, the dejections and rejections, marriages and grandchildren, deaths and losses.

The years roll on and I am in our Allahabad house, desolate and discarded with crumbling walls, roofs ready to cave in (only a few rooms livable) and our childhood haven is in disrepair.

Something was tugging me again and again to the house. Our family priest's voice echoes in my ears: "The Tulsi (holy basil) bush in the courtyard will wait for family to return to pay obeisance to your *janam bhumi* (land of birth) and your *karma bhumi* or land of action." I told him then that I did not believe in his mumbo-jumbo.

In Hindu mythology the Tulsi plant is the holiest of all plants with Brahma the creator god residing in its branches, other Hindu gods in its stems and leaves with the holy waters of River Ganga flowing through its roots. The Vedas bless the upper part of its branches. One who cares for the plant, generally the woman of the house, gains salvation. Mother had cared for the plant as long as she could. Maybe the priest was telling us that Tulsi represented our mother and that she wanted us to return home. We were late.

Six months later, still weak from surgery, I was on a flight to Allahabad for a last look at the 1950s sprawling bungalow appropriately named "Ram Niwas" (my father's name was Ram after our Hindu God Ram). The house was under the scanner and to be demolished as the three remaining siblings (two younger brothers and I) decided to let it go.

I look up at the crumbling façade and see my mother's tender face. I ask for forgiveness for childish tantrums, for not understanding her pain, expecting her to be constant in our lives, sacrificing her pleasures and needs at an age, thirty-eight years, when girls today straddle the world. She was educated and meant for bigger and better things, not just a widow with five brats.

I wanted to be left alone, to walk the rooms, the lightless corridor, the courtyard (the Tulsi shrub was still there waiting for us), the sprawling lawns that once bloomed with exotic lotus, dahlias and roses, where parents entertained and we celebrated our birthdays, where my brothers played cricket and badminton refusing to let me join in. I walked every space where the five of us had shared our sicknesses (measles, typhoid, mumps one after another), had fought and played, hiding in our parents' bedroom with its canopied beds. I looked up to the terrace hoping to see the 'three laughing ghosts' smiling down on me.

I remember it being a peak summer of hot winds a week after father's death in June 1960. Since air conditioners were non-existent in this small town, we slept in the courtyard in mosquito-netted beds. I happened to look up at the terrace parapet and there they were... the three white and puffy faces. I was scared and hid my face with my sheet. A few minutes later I peeped and there was no one. I did not utter a word to my brothers.

Childhood memories are chimeric and no matter how hard we hold onto them they have a tendency to merge into the present.

Finally, I was at peace with myself after the last walk through the complex. I stood under our favorite mango tree as homage to our gardener friend and could hear him, "Baby, you will not get more." The rose bushes had long dried and so had the lotus, though the swings and the slide were there. Tentatively, helped by my husband, I sat on the swing. A gentle push and my curly hair returned.

The house was sold; the umbilical cord severed. We were on our own now with no links to bind us except for blood and memories.

Pilgrimgirl
Jana Remy

We all have those moments where one small step is taken and as a result everything else that follows is changed. For me that step was a warm fall afternoon when I was returning home from picking up my son from kindergarten, driving our small green station wagon down a major thoroughfare and impatiently waiting at a stoplight to turn left. Both of my children were buckled tightly into their car seats and we were driving home as we did every day, making the two right turns and one left turn and then parking in the small lot outside of our condo. The routines of our days were predictable and comfortable, routines to keep my young children entertained, safe, and fed while their Dad worked at the office. But as I sat at that stoplight waiting for the light to turn a digital marquee across the street caught my eye. It was our local community college on the corner of the intersection, announcing with flashing green letters: "Fall Registration Now Open."

On impulse I made an immediate right turn into the parking lot of the college instead of driving another block to our housing complex. I followed some arrows to the administration building, and parked in front of it. I pulled the double-stroller out of the trunk of the car and lifted the children into it and headed towards the Registrar's Office. I decided that I would look into what it would take to enroll in a class. Though I had graduated from college six years earlier I had never sought employment or used my undergraduate degree for paid work. My academic skills were dormant, but not gone. When I saw that sign announcing enrollment I felt a longing for something besides my predictable routines. I liked my life as a caregiver and wife, but I had a strong sense that there were some greater possibilities in my future. Combined with those feelings was a sense of my own untapped capacity—as someone who had lived with a visible disability for most of my life, having lost my right leg to bone cancer at a young age, I had always struggled to find employment and thought little of my prospects for being more than a mother. But I also knew that I was missing a leg and not my brain, and that I was hungry to learn more about the world, about literature, about others. I had a strong sense of wanting more even if I didn't yet know what that "more" was.

It was just a few weeks later that I cleared the dishes from the family dinner table one evening and then grabbed my purse, a spiral-bound notebook, and a copy of the campus map, and headed out the door for a long walk in the dark. I meandered through an orange orchard between our condo complex and the community college, entering at the back of the campus and standing under a streetlight to turn the map this way and that to locate the building where my class was to be held. I had enrolled in a late evening French conversation class, thinking that I might refresh my memory from having studied French in high school. As I walked through the rows of buildings I felt the layers of everyday self peel away, slipping off the role of mother, shedding the layer of dutiful wife, and entering that classroom where I would speak of my desire to eat cheese in Paris: *Je voudrais un sandwich camembert et je veux visiter* à *Paris.* The class was taught by a feisty petite Madame who needled me with questions, praised my grammar skills, and repeatedly insisted that I speak louder so that everyone could hear me. Before long that trek through the orange trees was the treasure of my week, a time that I could speak with my own voice.

The next semester I enrolled in two classes, keeping my French conversation class and adding a literature course about pilgrimage narratives. The first day of the class the professor introduced the texts that we would be reading: *Gilgamesh, The Odyssey,* and others. She then asked us to write a short in-class introduction paper about ourselves answering the question, "Are you on a journey?" As I wrote, I decided that I was on a journey and that it had started the day that I registered for that French class. But even as I also wrote that, I realized that I was unsure of where I was headed. So much of my life so far had been predictable from the framework in which I'd been raised: I was Mormon which meant marrying young and being a mother. I'd knelt at the marriage altar at age twenty-one and was soon pregnant. When I graduated with my bachelor's degree later the next year, my husband held our six week-old son while I walked across the stage to receive my diploma. I left the ceremony early to nurse the baby, sitting on a blanket in a grassy field outside of the rows of chairs for family members, listening to the calling of names drone on from the loudspeaker as my hundreds of classmates crossed the stage as I fed my baby. I had believed then that the earning of the degree was of far less importance than the nurturing role I would play in my family, to my husband and to all of the children that we hoped would soon follow.

I began blogging about the same time that I enrolled in that first French class. With my professor's question about being on a journey running through my mind, I took the online alias of *Pilgrimgirl*. Writing online to an imaginary audience felt strangely familiar to me, as I had always been a journal keeper and a letter writer. I loved the feeling of pouring out my thoughts on a page of brightly-colored stationery. My blog had a bright purple banner across the top of the page. My early entries were about my vegetarianism, gardening, and my abiding fondness for Mr. Rogers. It was hardly the stuff of an epic journey, but I could feel that my steps were now carrying me somewhere important. Just like I could be my true self when I was in the classroom, I found my own voice through writing online.

It was 2002 when I started my blog, which was when the genre was new and there were very few of us pouring out our hearts online every day. The small online world allowed me to find people like myself easily, and I began to form strong virtual friendships with others who shared interests in books, in hobbies, and in experience. Most memorable for me was when I became acquainted with Sara, a woman living in Concord, Massachusetts, who blogged about adopting a wandering kitty, who posted photos of the squirrels who spirited away peas from her garden vines, and who began mailing me small treasures via parcel post, the first of which was a handmade scarf of blue-purple wool. But most importantly, she shared a body and an experience like mine—she was also an amputee due to cancer and was bold about sharing online what her life was like missing a leg. I had never had a close friend who had cancer or shared my disability experience. The bright spot of every day was seeing Sara's avatar show up on my screen—her image was not a photo of herself but of a large ripe heirloom tomato. That tomato became the favorite part of my day as we carried on comments back and forth on whatever topic we had happened to be writing about.

We met in person when I happened to be on the east coast for an anniversary trip with my husband. The three of us ate sandwiches together on the banks of Walden Pond and I realized the comfort of finally finding someone who was more like me than anyone I had ever met before.

As the years followed we both blogged and commented on each other's sites while our community expanded to include a cadre of women who had similar experiences: breast cancer, terminal illness, a wicked sense of humor. These women became my tribe and my family as I applied for and was accepted into a PhD program, as I walked away from my Mormon faith and was then abandoned by my Mormon community, and as I began traveling solo.

When Sara's cancer returned in her brain she had surgery and we hoped that she had licked it. But when it returned again I flew back east to see her, not knowing whether she would even be strong enough for a visit. She was and it turned out to be a postcard-perfect fall day in October. She suggested that we rent a canoe and paddle leisurely down the Concord River. We were such an unusual pair, two thirty-something women who were both missing their right leg. Sara wore thick blue suspenders clipped to her sweatpants, having lost so much weight to cancer that she had no other way to keep her clothes hanging on to her thin bones. I did most of the paddling as she sat in the canoe and enjoyed the rusts and yellows and browns of the trees along the shore. I let us drift along lazily for a long while as we listened to the birds. The light reflecting on the water was so bright that it was impossible to see what lay ahead of us.

After bringing the canoe to shore she suggested we eat pasta at a nearby cafe. The great heaping bowls of noodles smelled heavenly after an afternoon of paddling. Sara twisted the noodles around her fork but dozed off before she ate any of them. I dropped her off at home, an old white wooden house with tall paned windows. It was the last time I saw her and the last time she left her house. The treasure of that day together would hardly compensate for how hard every day was after that without seeing her tomato avatar appear on my screen. I know now that she knew me in a way that no one else had before, and no one else would. Our bodies matched like two paper dolls cut from the same one-legged pattern, and I knew I would not find another again whose experience would be as familiar as my own.

Not long after Sara's death I posted a blog entry that would shock my family and friends, announcing that I was splitting with my husband of nineteen years. It was titled, "Separation (or some big changes ahead for our family)" and immediately there were dozens of friends reaching out expressing shock and concern. Up to that point I had lived my life through my blog for nearly ten years, posting daily about my family, academic aspirations, garden, poetry, and anything else that came to mind. While I would not say that it was my blogging that led to my divorce, in hindsight I think there is a strong argument that it might have been the biggest reason why we split. With the decision made more than ten years before to register for a French class, I not only took a first step on my journey towards academia and towards finding a welcoming online community, I took the first step in leaving the expectations of my family that I would be a lifelong caregiver and wife. That day I became *Pilgrimgirl*, a traveler seeking her own destiny. I discovered that I could be more than a mother, I learned the fulfillment of an academic life, and I widened my circle to include many people that supported me and *knew* me in ways that my husband did not. We had married so young and when we made that choice I hadn't yet known who I was, and when I did find myself I realized that who I was no longer fit with who my husband was, and I also knew that I could carry my children along on their life journeys without needing their father to help me.

I blogged the separation, I blogged the divorce, and I blogged the thrilling moments of beginning my very own life. As the end of my marriage coincided with the beginning of a new year, I set the following goals for that year and for my new (solo) life:

So this year my goal is to fall in love each and every day.
I'll fall in love with flowers
fresh bread
and cheese and Muscat grapes
the sounds of slow trains on tracks
and the scent of your sun-warmed skin
wizened tree trunks
painting with bold color
and writing final drafts
the sensation of clinging to high cliff walls
and skiing down powdery slopes
my plane landing on unfamiliar runways
Smiling
and sand between my toes
bright morning light reflecting off the water
and late-night skies full of stars.

This year I'll be wholly and completely in love with the present moment, and at the same time in love with every step of the journey that I'm taking to accomplish my long term goals.

This is it, my friends. I'm so excited for what lies ahead....[1]

---

1   Jana Remy, "I Love, and the World is Mine," Jana Remy (blog), February 2, 2011, http://janaremy.com/2011/02/09/and-the-world-is-mine/.

It would only be a few months later that I would cross the stage and be hooded with a velvet gold and blue collar to mark the earning of my doctoral degree. There were thousands of people in that arena on that day and there was a huge eruption of cheer from the two rows of people that were mine, those who knew that I was marking the end of a journey of more than a decade of academic pursuit that had begun with that day of pushing my children into the Registrar's office in a stroller. My son had just graduated from high school himself a few days before my ceremony. My daughter would follow suit two years later.

It might not be surprising that by the time I walked across that stage, my blogging had become a rare event and not a daily one. Occasionally I would post travel photos or a few thoughts about whatever books I was reading. However, after a while I stopped renewing my "Pilgrimgirl" domain name. I didn't feel like Pilgrimgirl anymore, so I migrated my thousands of blogposts to a subdomain of my professional portfolio domain at janaremy.com. I didn't want all of that content erased, but I also realized that the musings of those years no longer reflected who I was. Because I was no longer on a journey with an unknown destination. I had arrived.

And the Spirit Goes On
Jie Tian

I arrive, standing on a cliff under arching oak trees, overlooking the Warm Springs Dam and Lake Sonoma. It is late spring. A strong wind still breathes out the chill of a northern cold. Soft white puffs sail in the air. Pink and white buckwheat florets sway in the wind. Massive clouds are migrating. The sun shines on the new oak leaves. *Cisq ghale*—"beautiful tree"— is the Kashaya Pomo word for oak tree.

There is beauty all around me—the deep blue water, the invigorating chaparral hills, and the clear sky. Inside me, I feel my body's grief. The damming of the Dry Creek and the Warm Springs Valley creates Lake Sonoma in 1983. The damming causes a permanent loss of habitat and plant materials for native Pomo peoples that once inhabit this area in California. Mabel McKay, world renowned basket weaver and healer of the Lolsel Cache Creek Pomo tribe, her healer companion Essie Parrish of the Kashaya Pomo tribe, and people of other tribes cut willow branches and redbud barks on the hills and collect sedge roots in Dry Creek—the last marsh suitable for their growth, before the valley is completely submerged several hundred feet under water.

I know Mabel's story by heart now, from Greg Sarris' magical book, *Mabel McKay: Weaving the Dream*.[1] Mable is "prepared" and "trained" for her spiritual role as a healer and artist from childhood, without her knowing at the beginning. The spirit calls to her. She has to doctor and weave, or die. The spirit teaches her basket weaving and teaches her songs for doctoring

---

1 Greg Sarris, *Mabel McKay: Weaving the Dream* (Berkeley, CA: University of California Press, 1997).

and songs for calming the plants while out digging. Each of her baskets is a miracle. The Smithsonian collects her works. Museums hold special exhibitions in her honor. Famed universities invite her to lecture. Foreign dignitaries desire to meet her. But she is not lured by fame or power and remains true to her cultural ways and values and the teachings of the spirit.

I have wanted to pay homage to Mabel McKay and visit Dry Creek for some time now. I arrive, on June 1, 2019, twenty-six years and one day after Mabel McKay's death on May 31, 1993. My grief is not restricted to this habitat, or to Mabel's story alone. It is a grief that permeates wherever I go on this North American continent. I hear the bygone voices of native ancestors. I grieve for their tragic fate under colonialism, conquest, genocide, and invasion of their homelands by waves of colonizers. It is a cellular grief, it is an atmospheric grief, eating at me, as I see what is beneath the surface—former sacred land turned into highways, agricultural fields, shopping malls, factories, office buildings, nuclear sites, and tucked-away toxic waste dumps.

In a circuitous journey trying to sort my own orientations as an artist and maker, I migrate, seek teachers, and look for a tribe I can call my own, after leaving China, a land that was once "half-colonial" under Western imperial forces and torn apart by its own internal turmoil and revolution. I might have inherited a psyche of helplessness or powerlessness, typical of a people that have lost freedom and autonomy, under the rule of power, for any length of time in its history. In this long journey, I am also incredibly blessed and grateful to have had the opportunity to migrate. I am transplanted in America. I am graciously received in America. I have my fights with America. I can't say that I have acclimated. Not until I find Mabel McKay. After a quarter century, grieving and drifting in America.

I have some peace now and I have some sense of an orientation now, after I find Mabel McKay. I have secretly taken on Mabel as my own tribal ancestor and teacher. As I slowly piece together my life, I ask myself the same question that the spirit asks Mabel. *What are you put on earth to do*? Though no spirit whispers to me, I devise one for myself, almost like a child's play, when I was young. A writer! An artist! So I can express in freedom. My own preparation for this call is almost as dramatic and torturous as Mabel's: screams at night, nightmare, insomnia, fever and fatigue, a decimated young girl's body. I want to run away from this onerous call. I am sick when I do. Like Mabel, I have to do it, or die.

Seeing similar struggles playing out in Mabel's body anchors me. It even gives me comfort and assurance. Ours are haunted and holocaust bodies once, rescued from the graveyard of history. Mabel is the last healing doctor and basket weaver of her tribe. She is called to heal her people from the new cultural diseases of alcohol and dope that plague them. I am the only one of my generation to leave my family and my ancestral land. I must live to tell the tale. And first, I must heal myself, drawing on all the resources from memory and what I'd encounter on my journey.

I have drawn strength from Mabel's versatility and resilience, as a worker, maker, healer, and master basket weaver, all in one and all her life. Mable works at odd jobs washing and ironing white people's clothes with her grandmother, Sarah, at restaurants, at carnivals, at seasonal fruit-pickings. She cuts fruits at a cannery for over twenty years before her retirement. I cannot compare her displacement with my own: not the intensity, not the scale, not the degree of decimation. The persistence of her spirit and the spirit of her people teaches me to hold fast to life, to a community.

I gradually gravitate toward a vision, a union that Mabel's life illuminates for me. This vision unifies art with the natural world, unifies art with respect for the earth, and unifies the purpose of art with the materials and the intent of art-making. At Dry Creek, I witness a deviation from this beautiful vision. A lake made to enhance private property value and to support the agriculture and viticulture takeover of the former native land. Below *Cisq ghale*, I see the immovable, impermeable dam. Across the dam, a large dock for recreational boats to launch and moor. Fences up on the cliff and elsewhere. At Stewart's Point where Dry Creek meets Warm Springs Creek, wired fences are erected and government signs bar entry to the dam. Behind the crisscrossed wire, I hear water rushing in the creek, I see clouds moving above.

Perhaps, the ochre rocks on these hills also remember the history and the protests against the construction of the dam. The passing winds too would remember. Certainly, the native peoples remember. How the basket-weavers gather from nearby counties to protest, to try to salvage some sedge from the creek, to transplant them so the materials survive, so their culture and tradition continue. In her old age, Mabel McKay is brought to the protest, Sarris tells. *She stands against the giant yellow Euclid earthmover, less than a third of the height of its front tire.* A shameful chapter in the history where power is once again abused and used against a people who have already been driven out of their homeland, a people who have lost the freedom to migrate, hunt, and gather from their inland homelands to the coast.

When I ask again of what I am put on earth to do, I come into focus. Not to an isolated point of concentration, but rather a natural continuum, an ecology. I am seeking to recreate an ecology of making in my own practice: an ecology of interrelatedness. As a writer, can I make my own paper? Can I make my own ink? Can I make my own book? Can I dream different book forms? Can I open my own press? Can I grow or gather the materials for my making? My answer is yes and yes and yes. After the protest and loss at the Dry Creek, young native people start a nursery as part of the Ya-Ka-Ama Pomo Learning Center—a refreshing reimagining of what a learning center is— to preserve native plants for future generations of basket weavers.

I want to practice in an ecological community. And I start a garden. I incorporate the native, the medicinal, and the spiritual elements into the garden. I want to revive a sense of the native in the small parcel of land that I have come to inhabit, as a latecomer. To lean onto the land, to live close to the beings of the natural world, and to experience a sense of interconnectedness. *Artemisia californica*. Purple sage. Monkey flower. Yarrow. Yerba Buena. Blue-eyed grass. Desert marigold. This is a beginning. This is a natural garden and a healing garden. And I will have materials for ink and dip pen. I will gather and harvest, slowly and patiently, and I will make paper. Words will come out from the land too. I will adhere to the principles of the natural world and return natural materials to the earth. I co-join the metamorphosis.

Perhaps this is the most radical feminist work that I can do—to tend the earth, to tend the natural materials for my making, and to be intentional in my making. And I set out to learn, to relearn—and to gain intimate working knowledge of plants, animals, insects, the weather, the cycle of seasons, the stars and the planets. Perhaps this way, I will learn what making really is. And to experience freedom and interdependence as an artist. As the spirit says to Mabel—*I'll show you what to make for each person. Each of your baskets has a purpose. Each has a rule.*

Towards evening, the fog rolls in from the coast, hovering in the sky, thick and expansive like a floating mountain range. I remember a day when Greg Sarris drives Mabel from Santa Rosa to the Kashaya reservation to meet Essie Parrish for their spirit conversation. Enveloped in a primordial fog, Mabel sings a fog song, and the fog slowly lifts for them. Mabel dreams and lives the Dream. Her world as well as her baskets are alive, living, and magical.

As I come to Dry Creek to grieve and to memorialize Mabel McKay, I also feel an opening in me for healing, for hope. I can only imagine my art and my making to be living and magical. I can learn to pay respect to the earth and to have the right relationship with all living beings. And to make with a purpose. My journey is transformed from elegy into song. As I drive back along the Dry Creek Road to Healdsburg, I still see light illuminating the new oak leaves in the sun. *Cisq ghale*— the beautiful tree—thrives. Sarris' story revives me and connects me to Mabel McKay's Dream world. *It's the same. It's right here. It goes on.*

An Elemental Journey

Annie Knight

Then there are the dreams in which we open ourselves up to other people, dreams in which we find that the words and gestures, the crude and indirect ways of our waking life are not necessary. That we can be touched more directly. That we can listen and see better.

The Kin of Ata Are Waiting for You by Dorothy Bryant[1]

I found myself living a whole new life on a Pagan commune in New Mexico, 23 years ago. Having just graduated from high school, I was ready for something new. My intuition screamed and pushed at me from inside to fly far away and land somewhere new.

My memories of this place and time can't be contained by a linear timeline. Instead, a patchwork of profound moments from this experience are what I have to share. These moments were initiations and "firsts" mixed with magic and awkwardness. They helped build my core that bows down to nature, builds ritual into my daily life, and seeks ways to be in community with others. In my recount of these moments, the elements Water, Earth, Fire, Air, and Aether serve as thematic markers. This structure allows me to

---

1   Dorothy Bryant, *The Kin of Ata Are Waiting for You* (New York, NY: Random House, 1971), 191. [An incredibly influential book during this time in my life that taught me about the intersection of dreaming and waking life and how these realities can exist for us harmoniously—something I definitely experienced during my time in New Mexico.]

encapsulate the most meaningful pieces of my journey. (The names of the people in this story have been changed with respect to their privacy.)

At the time, I was seeing J, who previously lived on the commune. I daydreamed as he spoke about its natural hot springs, self-sustaining gardens, and simple living spaces surrounded by trees and mountains. It became the ideal place for the transformation I was seeking. Having only been exposed to passing Pagan references in my Catholic upbringing, I became intrigued by this new type of spirituality. My imagination fueled my need to move on, making the final months of high school drag even more. I planned to leave right after graduation and save as much as I could from my job at a local coffee shop. My parents' nervousness and trepidation had little impact on me. To their credit, they did their best to show support for my inevitable flee. Over time, I found gratitude for their faith in me to come out safe on the other end of this experience. As I packed for my trip, I made a deal with them that I'd be back in a month—a compromise that seemed to offer enough time to disconnect and fully immerse in the new and different.

Air

Sitting next to J on the plane as it took off from Ontario, California, to Albuquerque, I re-played scenarios of New Mexico. My visions of naturescapes and freedom were interrupted by Albuquerque's city elements that met us when we landed. J's friend, Riley, picked us up at the airport. He had lived on the commune for some time. The three of us with our waist-long hair, worn t-shirts, ripped jeans, and beat-up hiking shoes jumped into Riley's van to get away from the city as quickly as possible. My fears of not being accepted faded as I hopped into the van.

The freeway turned into a lingering, red-rock lined highway. It snaked through winding mountain roads. Nostalgia took over, comparing these mountains to the San Bernardino mountain ranges I grew up with, going on day hikes, summer camping trips where I watched stars fill up the night sky, and inner tubing adventures with my sisters and cousins on snowy days. I later learned we were driving along stolen land of Native Pueblo tribes, including Jemez, Tewa, and Keresan peoples.

This lens of new experience intensified the scenery around me. I was awestruck by the tiniest of pebbles lining the road. Watching the trees blur by while J and Riley caught up, my quiet excitement stirred up a strange sense of self. I found myself outside my body, watching the ride along this lived-in van, moving toward a place I knew little about. Trying on this new self for the first time, I floated outside my familiarities with an awkward, wider wingspan.

After a few hours, we turned onto a road that took us deeper into the mountains. The tree groves thickened and closed in on us like a shield. A stream flowed alongside the road with its clear water rushing over its light brown, rocky bottom. A lingering odor of hard boiled eggs creeped up my nose, as Riley asked if I could smell the sulfur. He explained how it flowed underground, adding to the healing properties of the local mineral springs.

At the commune space, there were no fences marking the property. There were patches of gardens and trailers surrounding the central house expanding to the nearby hillsides. It was an open space where folks could come and go. Some nights, while hanging out around the fire pit, headlights of arriving cars with their tires crunching over the dirt road stirred our peaceful, starry-sky cocoon.

A few days after we arrived, I woke up with an overwhelming urge to hike by myself up one of the surrounding hillsides. A cool breeze smoothed the skin of my tank-top covered shoulders as I watched my feet move across the trail's dirt floor with scattered rocks and leaves. I walked toward the sun not caring where the path took me. The warmth poured between my eyes and spilled down my chest and spread over my belly. I tasted the subtle smells of trees, plants, and dirt. I inhaled that air, it filled my throat and worked its way through my lungs. As I climbed higher, the deep blue sky seemed to draw closer and brighten between the treetops. I looked back to see the house and trailers on the commune space shrink and then disappear.

Further into my hike, I realized I was completely surrounded by trees. I found a rock to sit on. I ran my fingers over the rock's rough nooks, remembering prior hikes I had taken with other people, relying on their sense of direction. Here I was, left to my own sense of direction, and left to choose how to spend this time on my own. I didn't leave any markers along the way to guide me back. A brief twinge of fear surged through me. The fear passed and I embraced the time in the thick of the trees. I was where I should be. I studied the trees, and they looked back at me. Like coming face-to face-with a crush, I stared at their beauty feeling like I couldn't match what they had to offer.

I brought my flute with me. Even though I was alone, I found a new kind of audience with the trees and the creatures living in them. Back home, I only played for people during band performances or practicing in my room. To ground myself, I blew a simple, midrange D across the hole of the mouthpiece. The note resonated with an oscillating energy that shook me. The sound took its time before it lost momentum, bouncing off the trees, rocks, and mountainside. When it was quiet again, I heard a deeper layer of sounds. The trees swishing in the light breeze, bird calls at varying pitches, and tranquil water flowing in the distance. The bright sun shining through the trees amplified these pure sounds. As I kept playing, I felt my breath sync with the breeze. I paid attention to how the air flowed through me, circulating through my diaphragm. My energy rose with the pitch of the notes, and a headiness took over mixed with feelings of luck and gratitude.

Earth

During one of our daily hikes, J took me to a hillside referred to as Crystal Mountain by the regulars at the commune. Sparks of light beamed from the hillside as we approached it. Up close, large pieces of quartz peeked out through the loose dirt. As my hands grazed the dirt, more pieces spilled out of hiding. "Just hold it in your hand for a while," J explained. "Its energy protects against negativity."

While cupping one of the pieces in my dirt-caked hands, I closed my eyes. The warmth radiating from the quartz spread up my arms. Holding it tighter, the calm energy flowed through my entire body. I went outside myself again. Behind my closed eyes, I saw me, steeped in the dirt of the mountainside, face toward the sun, holding this earth treasure to my heart.

We continued exploring the dirt. We sifted through and admired the quartz pieces we found in silence. I thought about healing powers, wondering if I could ever truly understand what they mean. Physically connecting to the minerals and rocks of the land became a daily occurrence during my walks. Not only did I experience the power of holding them in my hands but I learned how they could be used as tools and symbols during rituals.

During preparations for a sweat lodge ceremony led by local elders, I helped Dee, a self-identified Lakota Native, gather large grandfather rocks that would be used to help create the steam during the ceremony. She explained their significance for the ritual and how to handle them with respect. I followed Dee's lead, placing the rocks gently into the fire pit in a circular pattern. As Dee went on to explain why we were using lava rocks with their propensity to hold heat, I traced one of the rock's rough texture with my fingers and felt its deep redness.

As we continued our preparations, Dee asked if I thought I'd ever be doing something like this. I wasn't sure how to answer her question. Dee sensed the uncertainty of my pause and continued to carry the conversation. She described the rules of the ceremony based in honoring the tradition and spoke about participants' safety. She detailed how elders spent years learning from their elders in how to lead the ceremony. As Dee's explanation wound down, she said something that stays with me still: "It's important to be invited as a guest." I took the pointedness of her words as advice. I couldn't articulate it at the time, but Dee's advice helped me understand that I was an outsider being invited into something sacred. As a white person it was not an inherent right to attend.

Sitting in a circle with others from the commune in the steam-filled lodge, sweat streaming down our bodies, I listened with intention to the words and songs of the elders leading the ceremony, watching their actions and taking their cues. I watched the steam rise up from the smoldering grandfather rocks. The hiss of the water being poured over the rocks intensified the swelling heat of the small enclosure. Sweat weighed down my hair while soaking my back and face. I tasted the salty drops that fell down to my lips and wondered on an unfamiliar abstract level about what was being drawn out of me. This thought pulled me through the synesthetic reactions I had to the words of the songs and the prayers, manifesting into intense feelings of humility and gratitude for this ceremony I was being allowed to participate in.

As we stepped out of the lodge the chill of the dusk air stung my entire body, working its way through me. The chill split me wide while the clean air I breathed in filled me with purity and newness. As we closed the ceremony, sitting together on two logs outside the lodge, Dee's advice about the invitation to the ceremony came back to me. Her words planted a seed in me that continues to root down over the years when facing my legacy as a white person with an ancestry that colonized this country. Dee's words are one of my daily reminders to continue to check my own complicity in it all and work to do better.

Fire

Sitting around the fire pit at night was a regular occurrence at the commune. The pit was located down the hill from the trailer I stayed in with J, and served as a regular gathering space where we talked, played music, did rituals, and wondered together at the stars. Perhaps it was my introverted nature, but I'd often find myself reflecting inward or just feeling the energy of the different people. A part of me was in continuous awe that I was a member of this group. Sometimes the conversation would vaporize into the endless stars of the Milky Way sky haloing us. Sometimes I'd pay more attention to the shadows of the flames dancing across everyone's faces. Others outside the light of the flame entered the conversation circle as invisible voices coming from untraceable directions. One of these voices belonged to Maria, one of the regulars I'd shared soulful conversations with during my stay, and I looked up to her as a wiser, older sister.

On the late afternoon of Summer Solstice, our fire pit area was transformed by everyone's contributions of oak wood, quartz, wild flowers, candles, incense, hand-made rock formations, and drums for the evening's ceremony. An altar was set up on a large rock nearby, covered in various bright scarves underneath candles, a pewter dagger, and two chalices. The sun reflected off the metal rim of the chalices and blade of the dagger. As a group, we discussed how we wanted to open the ceremony and the closing of the circle. All I really knew about Summer Solstice was that it marked the first day of summer, though growing up in regularly sunny Southern California didn't help the day stand out for me in this way.

Maria told me about Solstice rituals she practiced while we sat together making flower chains. Soon after, the priestess leading the ceremony called us to join in a circle around the fire pit. As the priestess opened the circle by honoring the four directions, I remembered times I'd spent back home in the mountains and compared it to my current surroundings, holding hands with Maria and J on either side of me. The priestess chanted incantations about the cycle of life and how we connect with nature as our guide. Her incantations mixed with the crackling sounds of the bonfire. I noticed the fire went through its own cycles, from sparks to full flames to smoldering embers, as the ceremony continued while the sun set.

After the ceremony, we built another bonfire for the drum circle that went on through the night. Everyone joined in their own ways – drumming, chanting, dancing, and howling. I played my flute to the pounding rhythms and the movement of those dancing around the fire, taking sips of wine and beer from the chalices that circulated. Making my way back to the trailer that night, the quiet brightness of the stars kept the dream going.

Water

The promise of the natural hot spring pools carried Riley, J, Maria, and me up the steep trail leading to them. Plants and shrubs scratched our legs and loose dirt powdered us as we navigated the narrow, overgrown path. The afternoon sun seared our heads and backs, and sweat streaked our dusty skin. After hours of hiking, a quiet breeze passed through and chilled the back of my neck. Sounds of distant water flow worked their way through the shrub wall on our right. We quickened our pace at the excitement of getting closer. The trail's incline leveled off and delivered us to a magical realm of a mountain top view and multi-tiered springs. We stopped to take in the view of the surrounding trees, mountains, and searing blue sky.

Voices from another group soaking in the pool nearby brought me back from my daze. I watched their floating heads as they talked and laughed.

Walking toward the edge of the rock-scaped pool, I watched my reflection grow in the dark water. A light steam coming from the water danced around everyone as we greeted each other. Seeing how comfortable our new friends were with their naked and varied body shapes, I felt less nervous about stripping down. Nakedness wasn't the focus. The nervousness dissolved as I lowered myself into the warm water's bliss. My body entered a new realm. The colors and shapes of trees surrounding us sharpened in contrast to the pinking sky. Leaning my head against the pool's edge, I closed my eyes and listened to the falling water that spilled from another pool above us. A calming energy radiated through my body, similar to what I felt when holding the quartz, and I disconnected from the voices around me.

A bird's cry woke me. I wasn't sure if I had fallen asleep or wandered somewhere else in my mind. The person sitting next to me looked over and smiled, commiserating, "Yeah, I did that the first time too." The setting sun in the background illuminated their face. I saw a similar glow radiate through my hands when I raised them out of the pool and watched water drops fall from my fingertips. For a moment I didn't recognize my skin that looked unbelievably polished and smooth with this glow that seemed to mirror the sunset.

Aether

While packing my things on the last day of my stay, I stared at the flower chains, quartz piece, baggie of soil from one of the commune's gardens, and a trinket of the wood I learned to chop for the kitchen's potbelly stove. The strangeness of packing these things in a bag that would go with me away from this place set heavy in my gut. I began to fear that I might forget everything I learned here once I returned to my city life. I knew the change in pace, scenery, and people of returning home would hit me hard. Luckily, as I said my goodbyes to the new family I found here, I was reminded by their invitations to visit again. I didn't have to leave this place forever.

Cycles of nature and cycles of relationships occupied my mind for much of the trip home. My mind kept wandering back to a conversation I had with Maria about her relationship with Riley. I admired the way they shared their love for one another while respecting each other's individual paths. She'd be returning to school on the east coast that fall, and he would most likely stay on at the commune. I thought about what that looked like for me and J while imagining my own path that spread far beyond. I couldn't discern any specific scenarios, timelines, or plans. Wanderlust filled my senses, along with a vague understanding of there being a connection through it all — even as our plane landed in the summer haze of Southern California's smog. Since then, I've studied ways to build nature, ritual, and the variety of love I encountered during my New Mexico journey into my daily life. I feel it the most when I'm walking the river bottom near my home now, gathering rocks and fallen branches that feed my art and serenity. Over the years, the beauty and lessons of that magical commune have guided me through many decisions, moves, relationships, commitments to action, and soulful retreats.

I Didn't Expect This!: How Healing and Care Became a Part of My Black Feminist Journey in Academia

Amanda LaTasha Armstrong

What it means to be a Black woman was defined by society, contested by my family, drizzled into acquaintances and social interactions, and became a part of me. I took on this way of being until I got tired and started to ask who do I want to be in this world.

Amanda LaTasha Armstrong

I sat in my new therapist's office unnerved yet satisfied with my decision to make an appointment. Several weeks ago, I completed a writing assignment for one of my doctoral courses. Stress from expectations of producing a high-quality work turned my thoughts foggy and blended with quick heart beats and an upset stomach, leaving my body fatigued. Depleted by exhaustion, I slept for a few hours until I woke up mentally a little clearer and too exhausted to do anything else but work. As I progressed through my assignment, feelings and thoughts of "not being good enough," "needing everything to be perfect," and "trying to anticipate what my professors wanted" kept nagging at me, stunting streams of consciousness and disrupting my writing flow. After hours of struggle, I submitted the assignment and sat amongst papers dispersed on the floor in the residue of my fatigue. I decided this way of life no longer suited me.

I recounted this event to my therapist, explaining, "I decided to come here because I want to change. I've dealt with anxiety before and I want to address the reasons for my anxiety before it gets worse." For the duration of the session, we discussed my history of taking medication for anxiety and depression, some of the known reasons for my mental health struggles, and the stressors that emerged after I moved from Chicago, Illinois, to southern New Mexico to begin a Ph.D. program. As we talked through my experience of starting a doctoral program and expectations of how people *should* handle stress, I realized how much I confined myself to certain responses and reactions. Questions began to arise during our dialogue, such as: "What do I value?" "What do I feel?" "How did I want to live?" Searching my therapist's eyes, shoulders, and posture for acceptable answers, I hesitated to reply each time, filling the silence with stares at the ceiling. When our session ended, rather than having confident responses, I became aware I had not really asked myself those questions before. How I defined myself was unknown to me.

The days and weeks between therapy sessions, I spent hours writing and reflecting on my experiences, choices, and all the details that come with living. The stillness of the desert made me sit in the messiness of myself without the distractions of city life, family events, friend meet-ups, and professional gatherings. The lack of a Black presence in southern New Mexico allowed me to question my approach to life without the concern of societal and cultural expectations or the use of tactics that have allowed me to survive in a sometimes hostile world. At the same time, I simultaneously longed for Black culture and missed seeing members of my community on a regular basis. The vastness of the high desert provoked me to imagine a different life and its intense light made sunglasses my circadian companion, filtering the sun and the judgements of others, allowing me to sense what I needed and wanted.

Caring for myself is not self-indulgence. It is self-preservation, and that is an act of political warfare.
Audre Lorde, *A Burst of Light and Other Essays*[1]

---

1   Audre Lorde, *A Burst of Light: And Other Essays* [Kindle Edition] (Ithaca, NY: Firebrand Books, 1988), 130, Location 1702.

Taking the time to write, reflect, and process comments or questions posed during therapy made my habits and the language of my self-talk more apparent. During my upbringing and young adulthood, there were occurrences, in which my mind "went somewhere else." The present moment of being in the body and of the body was too daunting to comprehend or shocked me into unresolved questions. Suppressing emotions and diminishing my connection to my body and sensations protected and assisted me in enduring traumatic events and dealing with the intersectional oppressions that come with being a Black woman. I could escape to my mind to make sense of events or forget those too unpleasant to recall. While these habits helped me function and get through life, they also created a disconnection of fully savoring and perceiving the dimensions of moments and relationships with others.

With each therapy session, we processed my life, talking through alternative responses and generating options that worked for the Amanda into which I wanted to evolve. Rather than ignoring my feelings, sensations, or reactions, I acknowledged them, determined their cause, and paused. Sitting in the discomfort of learning about myself, I gathered small droplets of insight: "shift your energy around with physical movement," "take breaks," "be kinder to myself," and "build relationships with people who have similar values." Giving myself time and permission to think differently helped me determine how I wanted to proceed or respond in a way that aligned with my new values.

I began working out regularly as a part of my new life rhythm. Weeks when there were many assignments and projects to complete, I found it even more imperative to do some sort of cardio, strength training, and yoga to release my energy. I reached out to friends and family members more often, finding comfort in sharing our experiences, and learned how to be compassionate to myself. I was introduced to biofeedback therapy, where I learned how to use breath and time as a way of working through episodes of anxiousness. The present moment became a space where I could foster different ways of being through applying "tools" that served the evolving Amanda.

Times when I knew I would be in environments or around people where I did not feel emotionally or mentally safe or would encounter possible triggers for depression and anxiety, my therapist and I brainstormed additional strategies to put in my toolkit. We talked through ways for me to be safe, manage my responses, and maintain the level of contentment I had started to feel daily. My toolkit ranged, sometimes including visualization techniques or visiting places that fostered love, creativity, and appreciation, like parks, art museums, and used bookstores. The versatility of the toolkit allowed me to use a technique that worked for that particular context. Over time, I felt more confident in my ability to deal with unexpected situations and more attuned to the groove of my new life rhythm.

"...the pursuit of health in body, mind and spirit weaves in and out of every major struggle women have ever waged in our quest for social, economic and political emancipation."
Angela Davis, "Sick and Tired of Being Sick and Tired: The Politics of Black Women's Health"[2]

There was a particular lack of Black history and culture in the area of southern New Mexico where I had moved. Having relocated from Chicago where Black culture was an integral piece of the city, there were times when my ancestors and I seemed invisible and feelings of detachment and somberness lingered as I went on hikes, explored historic places, and visited casual dining spots. It wasn't until I moved to southern New Mexico that I realized how much I valued Black culture, missing the various nuances that came with living in a Black community and seeing the influence of African Americans on contemporary culture. Social media, online publications, academic articles, and video and phone conversations with family and friends became means of staying connected to Black culture. I surrounded myself with art depicting the softness of Black women to remind me of the complexity of our collective experience, showing our humanity, vulnerability, and beauty. I developed and nurtured relationships with other women of African descent who were having similar experiences of wanting to create lives, habits, and ways of being that nurtured them holistically (i.e. spiritually, mentally, physically, emotionally, and financially). In being a part of these online communities and building healthy sisterhoods, I felt encouraged to keep evolving and reimagining a new life rhythm.

---

2   Angela Davis, "Sick and Tired of Being Sick and Tired: The Politics of Black Women's Health," in *Black Women's Health Book: Speaking for Ourselves*, ed. E. C. White (Seattle, Washington: The Seal Press, 1990), 19.

As I developed a different way of life and discovered the benefits of taking breaks and maintaining healthy habits, guilt emerged. Statements and questions appeared in the same silence that nurtured my emerging holistic lifestyle: "This is taking too much time," "How do you know this is going to work; Do what you know," and "Do you think other doctoral students would be taking a break now?" Discussions with a few peers in the doctoral program magnified feelings of remorse even though therapy sessions assured me I was growing and expanding.

While these conflicting feelings and thoughts were occurring, I was taking a course with an African American woman professor who is a Womanist scholar. Throughout her course, she emphasized the importance of taking care of ourselves in the midst of our doctoral program and making time to do other activities. Boundaries was a theme she repeated, which also seemed separate from the expectations that came with being a doctoral student.

Additionally, she and a group of women professors hosted gatherings for graduate students who identified as women of African descent. At these gatherings, we talked about our experiences as women of the African diaspora in academia, celebrated our progress through our respective programs, and shared knowledge, resources, and insight. Often times, the professors recommended books by Black Feminist and Womanist scholars, whose works paralleled my challenges, epiphanies, and experiences, allowing me to feel connected to the past and present. Being around these women helped me continue to dismantle the image of being a strong Black woman and consistently question who I wanted to be. They along with mentors and colleagues of other cultural, gender, and identity groups helped me feel comfortable with my choice to heal, make holistic health a priority, and focus on how I can continue to improve.

"I have come to believe over and over again that what is most important to me must be spoken, made verbal and shared, even at the risk of having it bruised or misunderstood. That the speaking profits me, beyond any other effect."
Audre Lorde, *Sister Outsider*[3]

---

3   Audre Lorde, *Sister Outsider: Essays and Speeches* [Kindle Edition] (Trumansburg, NY: Crossing Press, 1984), 40, Location 591.

Therapy sessions continued for a few years, which allowed me to step back from situations and reflect. Being aware of who I wanted to be and my values shifted my questioning to: "Was I acting according to my values?" "What did I notice about this occurrence?" "Is there a pattern I am continuing?" "Is this how I want to live?" Even with this growth, I felt stuck. I could feel certain truths caught in my throat I was not ready to discuss. There were parts of my life I had minimized or thought I had healed. Eventually, I knew my freedom and continual evolvement was based on my ability to be fully honest with my life and confront those situations where I felt shame, guilt, and horror.

The development and expansion of my toolkit prepared me for a series of EMDR (Eye Movement Desensitization and Reprocessing) sessions. The desire to confront some of the most afflicting adversities of my life and approach healing in a new way both frightened and thrilled me. I spent months researching my therapist's references about EMDR along with praying about the idea before I agreed it seemed a worthwhile endeavor. In each EMDR session, I processed either a traumatic event or psychosomatic symptom I developed as an attempt to lessen the chances of future traumatic events. The intensity of each session often utilized so much energy I did not work for the rest of the day. Progressing on my dissertation became substituted with hours of resting, utilizing one of the strategies in my toolkit, or engaging in an activity that fostered growth, healing, or pleasant feelings. Dreams became a way to resolve the residue of the memories discussed in each session, and writing became my mechanism for further processing and understanding myself and others.

I learned to be okay sitting in the unknown, committing to the unfolding of myself which comes with therapy, and letting go of the weight of trauma. Feeling more fully present in my body, emotions, and mind, I began asking myself, "Who is Amanda?" "Who did I come on this earth to be?" "Am I being my fullest self?" In this questioning, I felt free to discover Amanda and the intricacies of me. In acknowledging the truth of my life, I was able to see the true me, which I had never known.

"To be black means to have body and soul together. That is why, customarily, we used to define a 'together' person as 'having soul.' ...A marvelous thing happens when the body and soul are together, something that is the essence

*of who we've always been, and in our deepest nature still are: we care. To be
black means to care. About everything"*
Alice Walker, *We Are The Ones We Have Been Waiting For*[4]

In being honest and forthcoming during my doctoral journey about who
I was, what I wanted, and how I wanted to live, I have developed a clearer
sense of myself. Connecting to multiple facets of me has enhanced my ability to relate to other people, seeing similarities in our struggles, having compassion for life choices, and finding kinship in our values. Even though I
miss living in the city and amongst Black people, I know the healing work
I needed to do had to occur in New Mexico. I also realized I can nurture
Black Feminism within myself while living in an environment that I hav-
en't considered an epicenter of Black culture.

There were circumstances where I considered regressing and going
back to my old way of functioning because I knew it and it worked, and
I'm sure these types of occurrences will happen again. Yet, the desire for a
better life rhythm and the commitment to doing something new kept reappearing, as if higher beings and ancestors were telling me to keep going
on the path. Now, I am more present, using my intellect, senses, emotions,
and intuition to guide me through choices and notice the textures of moments. The intentionality of cultivating relationships, images, books, and
other materials and designing an adaptable "toolkit" have fed my soul, sustained my holistic approach to life, and helped me stay in alignment with
who I am, who I want to be, and my purpose.

---

4   Alice Walker, *We Are the Ones We Have Been Waiting For: Inner Light in a Time of
    Darkness* (London: Weidenfeld & Nicolson, 2007), 240.

The Beloved Thing
Elizabeth Kenneday

At age three I became obsessed with photography. The earliest coherent memory I have is of my mother pointing a square black box with a cyclopic glass eye at me. She has dressed me in a new outfit and faced me into the sun, which makes me squint. She is not happy with the squinting but my eyes hurt when I open them as she admonishes me to do. Some days later she shows me pictures of myself in my new outfit and I am mystified. What magic is this?

My fascination with cameras and what they were capable of doing stayed with me through childhood. After much pleading through the years I was finally given my own Brownie Starmite when I graduated from junior high school. I took pictures of everything around me. I dressed my friends up in costumes in an early "studio" mode, making images of their ridiculous antics. The only time I wanted to attend the rival high school was when I found out they offered photography classes and mine did not. I wanted to develop my own film and photographs—the darkroom seemed like some sort of alchemical wonderland and I yearned for that experience.

Advancing to a 35mm camera in college, I was at last able to study photography. I spent every open lab time I could in the campus darkroom—a more magical experience than I had imagined. The prevailing protocol then for learning photographic technique had been to emulate the Ansel Adams style of photography, which required training in the Zone System for exposure and development. While I was not keen on the tedium of the method, I did realize its value in providing consistency in my negatives, which was sorely lacking prior to those exercises. Though the Ansel Adams style was beautiful, and enormously popular, it was simply not *my* style. I wanted an approach to my photographic work that was both unique and personal.

The photography industry itself catered to men. Advertisements for professional cameras illustrated men exclusively using their products, a practice I pointed out to the Hasselblad Corporation when I was surveyed by them years later after being a Hasselblad owner for decades. I was probably not the only woman using a Hasselblad to speak out about this practice to them as later that year I received a poster featuring a woman behind one of their cameras. Even the language of photography was aggressive to my mind—*shooting* the subject, *capturing* the moment, *taking* the picture—sounding more like a military exercise than the joyful act of creation that I found it to be.

Teaching art at the university level, with a studio emphasis in photography, became my career goal. Academic photography was dominated by all-male faculties, as I was to discover. In fact, throughout my entire career I never worked with another full-time woman faculty member in a photography program. There were many full-time women faculty in the other studio disciplines, and several adjunct women faculty in the area of photography, but, as a full-time woman professor in my discipline, I often felt like a token appointment. This was particularly true when I started my career and, unfortunately, my decision making then was often affected in ways that now seem foolish to me, accommodating my colleagues rather than asserting myself.

In those early years, however, I was simply unaware of the numerous women who had used the camera as artists and professionals since its inception in the early nineteenth century. Women had been excluded, with atypical exceptions, from participation in fine art academies since their

Figure 1

Figure 2

establishment in Renaissance times. As the camera was considered a mechanical monstrosity not worthy of attention by that establishment when it appeared, women of the nineteenth century took to it with little concern for artistic conventions, creating innovative and expressive imagery. All of that was a revelation to me as I continued my studies.

One woman's work stood out to me from among the remarkable work of the pioneering 19th and early 20th century women photographers. The imagery of Anne Brigman combined the female body with nature in a way that blended them fully (fig. 1 shows Brigman's *Dawn*). I was astounded by

Figure 3

Figure 4   Figure 5

what I saw in those images: women in contemplative reflection, women in stormy turmoil, women emerging—all in nature (see fig. 2 of Brigman's *The Cleft of the Rock* and fig. 3 of her *The Bubble*). Specifically, they were set in the Sierra Nevada, a region I loved so well that I later served as an Artist in Residence and a Seasonal Interpretive Ranger in Sequoia National Park. Brigman's work was a revelation to me, and I began researching everything I could find about the artist who created such enchanting imagery.

Trained in drawing and painting, Brigman began working in the Pictorialist tradition of soft-focus photography that was meant to emulate painting, using her previous art skills in the manipulation of her negatives to attain her captivating compositions (see fig. 4 of Brigman's *The Dying Cedar* and fig. 5 of Brigman's *Death of the Cedar*). She would set out in summer on camping trips with her sister or a couple of other friends to Desolation Valley in the Lake Tahoe region, a daring venture for women alone in the early 1900s. With her camera in tow—the Beloved Thing, as she called it—she would pose herself and her friends as models in natural settings for her exposures, then worked in her studio in Oakland in the winters to finish her creations.

First exhibiting her photographs in the 1902 San Francisco Photographic Salon, Brigman received noteworthy acclaim. Alongside that exhibition was a showing of prints from the prestigious Photo-Secession, founded by the influential New York gallerist and photographer Alfred Stieglitz. Brigman began a correspondence with Stieglitz after being inspired by the works she saw in that exhibit, as well as in his legendary publication *Camera Work*. Stieglitz, in turn declaring that she had struck "a new note" in her use of the female nude in nature, inducted her into the Photo-Secession— the only West Coast photographer, male or female, to be so honored— and began showing her work at his Gallery 291.

Much has been written about Anne Brigman's use of the female nude and its function in her imagery, but the key to her appeal for me lies in her open, honest, and unafraid approach to her personal vision. In this she is often paired with her contemporary: modern dancer Isadora Duncan, who danced in diaphanous or no attire. Coincidentally, both women hailed from the Bay Area of California.

I see the movement in non-eroticized female nudity by women artists, particularly photographers, foreshadowed in the work and life of photographer Gertrude Käsebier. Unhappily married and dissatisfied with the constrictions of her cultural milieu, she developed a fascination with photography, beginning her photographic career in 1874. She worked primarily in portraiture, but her depictions of domestic life and motherhood were immensely popular. Attracting the attention of Alfred Stieglitz, she became a founding member of his Photo-Secession, and later in her career, she created an enigmatic image titled *The Bat*. In it, a nude female emerges from a rock cave with outstretched arms and "wings"—dark forms probably created by a shroud of some sort. The image dates from 1902, a year after the death of Queen Victoria.

Both Brigman's and Duncan's careers emerged as the Victorian Era ended, and while it would be simplistic to say that both women were using their bodies solely to express their desire for freedom from cultural constrictions as other factors were at play, I think both women exemplified the modern woman of the early twentieth century in this regard. Women were seeking to reveal and explore a true self apart from the roles set up for them in the Victorian Era, and both Brigman and Duncan utilized their mediums effectively to this end, creating enduring works of art.

Brigman's work clearly influenced Stieglitz himself when he began photographing his future wife, painter Georgia O'Keeffe, ten years later.

O'Keeffe is seen nude in his photographs, posed in ways that are reminiscent of elements in Brigman's compositions, often twisting her arms or her fingers in gestures resembling the twisted trees of the Sierra Nevada.

Georgia O'Keeffe was also utterly taken with Brigman's work when first introduced to it, and some of Brigman's compositional elements can be seen in her paintings as well. I sometimes wonder if the twisting and dead trees in some of O'Keeffe's paintings echo the emotion of Brigman's images of similar subjects, or whether O'Keeffe is perhaps reiterating her experience in posing for Stieglitz.

As the photographic trends began to shift away from the Pictorialist tradition, Stieglitz shifted with them. Brigman resisted following the new trends of the Group $f64$, dedicated to sharp-focus imagery. I admired her stance. I also admired that, after a brief stint in New York, she decided to return to the West Coast despite the fact there were more opportunities for artists in the New York milieu. She understood where she belonged for her work and her life.

I was to learn much more about Anne Brigman that intrigued me. She was a member of the Berkeley Bohemia, creating and participating in "dramas" that were popular at the time. She wrote poetry, publishing *Songs of a Pagan*, which combined her imagery with her poems. She became for me the ideal of a woman leading the fully engaged life.

I knew from experience that the photographer's original prints are so much richer than even the best reproductions. Subtle nuances of the original prints are lost in reprinting—the paper surface and color, shifts in contrast and, especially in the case of Anne Brigman's work that used manipulated negatives, the mark of the artist. I had to examine her originals.

A significant, though small, collection of Brigman's prints that was in general proximity to me was held at the Center for Creative Photography located on the grounds of the University of Arizona in Tucson. I applied for professional development funds from the institution where I was then a tenure-track professor to travel to the Center in 1992. In order to obtain the funds my application had to include research in the library and a more comprehensive viewing in the portfolio collections of several photographers' works—all of which would be appreciated, but my truest intention was to see original prints made by Anne Brigman's hands.

My husband and I set out on a road trip to Tucson during Spring Break. Once at the Center, I was almost giddy as I sat through the slow viewings of other photographic works of note—each set being brought in its own portfolio box and painstakingly placed in the viewing box by a white-gloved staff member—leaving the Brigman prints till the end so that I could savor them.

They did not disappoint. I was rapt as I regarded them up close, as artists looking at the work of their idols often do. I delighted to the characteristic Pictorialist softness of the edges and the areas that were blended by Brigman's deftness with negative manipulations. Moving back, I saw the beauty and the emotional resonance of women merged with their surroundings, responding to and reflecting the mood of their private worlds.

Unfortunately, the viewings were timed, and the prints were gathered up as caringly as they had been set out. My first pilgrimage ended as I watched the portfolio box disappear with the attendant down the hall. I left that viewing with a new sense of inspiration and faith in my own work, and a determination to impart that sense of excitement and confidence to my students, especially the women, in their photographic endeavors.

I was planning a second pilgrimage in 1995, when a male colleague decided the trip sounded like a splendid idea and he'd like to join me. As a junior faculty member I could hardly refuse his request, but I feared the pilgrimage would be diminished, and it was. During the portfolio viewings he seemed impatient, and his presence felt like an imposition as I attempted contemplation of Brigman's prints. Apparently, he was looking for a Spring Break vacation for he and his wife that would be partially funded by the college—not the sort of experience I sought. Completely frustrated, I vowed to return again under more satisfying circumstances.

I was able to make three more pilgrimages to Tucson over the next four years to view Brigman's prints, and each time my enthusiasm for her work—and for mine—were deepened and renewed. Following my last trip to Tucson I accepted a post at a new institution. I brought with me the self-assurance and joy I had gleaned from those five pilgrimages to Tucson to view the original works of Anne Brigman, who, in the act of using the Beloved Thing—her camera—established her place in the world, freed her from the constraints of the societal norms of her time, and allowed her to live life on her own terms. Her example establishes her firmly in my mind as an early feminist artist, inspiring those to come, including myself.

After retiring from academia, my husband and I moved closer to the Sierra Nevada, landing in Reno, Nevada. In a delightful surprise, the Nevada Museum of Art in Reno mounted an exhaustive retrospective of the work and life of Anne Brigman in 2018–19, featuring over 300 works culled from various sources as well as ephemera from her life.

Excited by the prospect of seeing previously unseen works and related material from her life, I visited the museum. Although it was heartwarming to see so many people discovering Brigman's work, it was difficult to have the transformative encounter I'd experienced in Tucson. The crowds were milling around with audio devices to hear the museum's commentary—effective ways to disseminate information, but difficult for quiet contemplation.

I made a decision to return another day when the museum first opened its doors. No one was yet in the galleries where Brigman's work was exhibited. I walked through all of the galleries—so many works I'd never seen before, favorites I wanted to revisit, and the letters, articles, and personal photographs of friends and family that were displayed. I was able to absorb all of it in my own time, gleaning new insights and rekindling my fascination for the woman whose photographic work and lifestyle so inspired me during my career.

Eventually a few more people trickled into the space. Then, after about an hour or so, crowds filled the gallery. I left the museum, having had the uplifting "pilgrimage experience" once again.

London. Lingering. Life.

Cass Hartnett

I recently took an online quiz that showed I have a ruminative personality. No wonder I like to think about London repetitively, to dwell there in my mind. Although I am walking around in Seattle, I am thinking about my visits to London, three in less than four years, at ages 49.9, 51, and 53. Each trip has had deep significance to me, especially the first, just days before my 50th birthday, my first venture outside the U.S. or Canada. At my undergrad college, a large percentage of students studied abroad for junior year. Not me. I was too busy trying to be a Big Feminist on Campus, taking classes in an emerging minor: women's studies. Making up for lost time, I have been taking in London's sights with the wonder of a teenager and the lived experience (and embodiment) of a middle-aged American woman.

It is my wife's job that launches me abroad. She's a psychology professor who offers an undergrad study away class, with London as the destination. Spouses are allowed on these trips as well. Here was my chance. By day, I am a librarian, and I frequently shake my head in disbelief that I have been so for over thirty years. Mostly I help people find government information, like Census figures and Congressional reports. But I am also the Gender, Women, and Sexuality Studies Librarian at my university, so I am still trying to be a Big Feminist on Campus. I once thought I was destined to be a singer-songwriter rock star, but I can still only play about three guitar chords. London is like one of those suspended guitar chords, the ones with a far-away sound. The chords that hang in the air waiting for your next down strum.

I remember my Delta flight descending into Heathrow for the first time as I watched the "follow your flight" feature obsessively on the in-flight entertainment system. We were over Ireland: land ho! It was the first land mass I had seen in hours, the Emerald Isle of which we sang in elementary school St. Patrick's Day shows, now a materializing reality. And here on the tiny map screen was a town labelled Limerick. A real place, Limerick. I looked out the plane window to see a deep cleft of the sea wending its way eastward into the green land mass, meeting up with the River Shannon in a place called Limerick, in County Limerick. I learned: they (those people over there) put a word like river or county *before* the place it describes. I was en route to England, where the grass and trees, which I thought might look different than anything I had seen before, looked normal, and people's backyards, which I had expected to be manicured, looked normal too, some even reassuringly messy.

Figure 1

One of my formative experiences that first time in London had to do with a true surprise. My college friend Susan offered me a meet and greet with a friend of hers who works near Buckingham Palace. I had been in town for four or five days now, and the pretense was that I would be able to see an unparalleled view of the Palace from her friend's office. It was only when I arrived that I learned that the friend, whom I will call Alan, worked directly with a member of the royal family. As if that weren't enough, the office held a sizable archive of records relating to royalty. Knowing that I am a librarian, Alan had arranged for the collection's expert curator to meet with me. She provided hands-on access to stunning artifacts leading back to the Fourteenth Century: an ancient map, records from the War of the Roses. The curator, trying to break the awkwardness of my incredulity, asked cheerfully, "Well, who is your favorite king? Everyone has a favorite king!" The question stopped me dead. Like most "ugly Americans," my knowledge of UK history and kings is quite lacking. I mumbled a response about the fascinating upheaval during the times of Henry VIII (he wasn't so nice to women).

My friend Wendy chuckled later that day when I recounted the "favorite king" question. "You should have said 'The Queen, of course.'" I could pick between Victoria, Elizabeth I, and the current queen, Elizabeth II. She, Elizabeth Alexandra Mary Windsor, is the longest serving monarch in British history, second behind her great-great-grandmother Victoria. The Queen's image is ubiquitous, and since I've spent 90% of my life living near Canada, I am accustomed to seeing her image on coins and bills everywhere.

The Queen's image calls to mind whiteness, colonialism, empire, strict gender conformity, and all that comes with it. But it also evokes longevity, fidelity to one's occupation, working motherhood, matriarchal rule, and a matriarchal *line*. Who is the American woman who might evoke the same sense of reverence from "her people," that feeling of wanting to say and do the right thing around her, not from blind protocol but of wanting to deserve the honor? During the time of Elizabeth II's reign, countries have changed profoundly in their relation to the Commonwealth—that's a sugar-coated understatement—and yet she has been a constant presence. In her nineties, she is a universal, albeit white and colonialist, crone. In her eyes, can humanity see reflected the latter 20th century and the new millennium?

My 2016 trip found me meandering through Hyde Park, following the unfollowable path of Diana, Princess of Wales. If I were to follow Diana's whole Memorial Walk, marked by metal rose medallions in the ground, it would stretch for seven miles through eight Royal Parks (fig. 1 shows Diana, Princess of Wales Memorial Fountain). The Walk culminates with a bubbling, human-made brook that runs in an endless circle in its granite-hewn river bed, a setting that instantly brought me in touch with something wistful. Who was this woman? She had an embodied life, but she was also the extension of international fantasy and hope, a collective yearning that can never be satisfied. With Diana's image so exploited by tabloids, the walk seems a fitting memorial. For once, we do not need to worry about what she looked like—how about where she walked? As visitors, we are welcome to dip our feet in this river-fountain, a natural spring that returns to the earth. It was too cold that day to bathe my feet in the water of Diana-remembering. But I had to stay there for a while, to listen to the water sounds, to think about women's lives. I connect it to other losses, a woman friend who died tragically, a beloved aunt, a young coworker who took her life, unable to push beyond eating disorders and depression.

＊ ＊ ＊

The curator back in the archive could have asked me who my favorite Prime Minister was, too—even my favorite female one. By the time of my third trip, I am learning about Theresa May. During my time there, she had a cabinet reshuffle. The education secretary, the Right Honourable Justine Greening MP was let go. Greening was in a lesbian relationship, a fact that the press seemed to mention in every article. I remember the tabloids publishing photos of her the day after her firing, out on her daily jog.[1] Another blonde woman followed down the street by paparazzi. And there I was in the narrative, consuming the photos over an English breakfast. What is it that we want to know about women?

In January 2018, I got to think about that question in some depth. I travelled back to London specifically to purchase feminist and queer literature for my library at independent bookstores, inspired by the tradition of feminist bookstores. I also wanted to visit places that would increase my professional knowledge of gender studies. I wrote about this experience in a newsletter for academic librarians, explaining the details of my acquisitions trip.[2] Donald Trump and Brexit were dominating the news, then President Trump made his "shithole countries" comments[3] and ridiculed the Mayor of London for the siting of the new American embassy.[4] Trans-Atlantic outrage was everywhere. Art and books featured pussy hats, the global womxn's marches enshrined in print and photos.

Feminist zines, comics, books and journals jumped off the racks at me, offering a fresh and vigorous take on queerness, people of color, disability studies, mental health, feminism, transculture, labor inequities, and

---

1   Andrew Pierce, "How Theresa's Showdown with Justine Greening Turned Ugly: Andrew Pierce Has the Inside Story on the Very Rocky Reshuffle," *Daily Mail*, January 9, 2018, https://www.dailymail.co.uk/news/article-5252775/How-Theresas-showdown-Jus-tine-Greening-turned-ugly.html.

2   Cass Hartnett, "Queerly Feminist Bookstores and LAM's in London: One Librarian's Awakening," *WGSS Newsletter: Women & Gender Studies Section*, Fall 2018, https://acrl.ala.org/wgss/wp-content/uloads/2018/10/fall2018_wgss_news.pdf.

3   "Donald Trump's 'Racist Slur' Provokes Outrage," *BBC News*, January 12, 2018, https://www.bbc.com/news/world-us-canada-42664173.

4   Nash Jenkins, "London Mayor Sadiq Khan: 'Donald Trump Is Not Welcome Here,'" *Time*, January 12, 2018, http://time.com/5100568/sadiq-khan-trump-london-embassy/.

Figure 2

gender identities stretched to a new dimension. Such humor and creativity. I fell in love with a comic artist, Natasha Natarajan/Chikaboo Designs[5], who captures and draws her everyday thoughts in a way I find entertaining and universally insightful (fig. 2 shows Natasha Natarajan's "To Be or Not To Be" from 2019, used with permission of the artist). Being removed from my natural surroundings, I felt free to really sit with this content, to drink it in, to be moved, shocked, educated. I remember the way that a bookshop owner's mother explained the thinking behind her daughter's store, New Beacon Books, specializing in Black Britain and global Black culture. "My daughter should really be here," she said, "you wouldn't believe some of the things she can find, and some of the books people bring us here." Colonialism became palpable to me with my newfound realization of having grown up in a former British Colony—I had known that since the second grade, but now I could feel it in my bones and could more easily wonder what this meant (and means) for South Asia, Canada, Australia, and so many nations of the Northern (and Southern!) hemispheres. American Empire wasn't created out of a void. We had rather perfect role models.

I took this latest trip at age fifty-three, still decidedly not a globetrotter compared to most of the young educated people around me. I became just as interested in what was going on in our hotel as I was in my work-related

---

5 See https://www.chikaboo-designs.com

destinations. I considered the lives of Athina and Silvia, the Greek women who served my breakfast daily and spoke of sending money home to their daughters. Athina and I took a liking to each other, and she was delighted that I am Cassandra and my name is Greek even if I am not. I wanted to study the rowdy female high school students on our hallway, a Spanish soccer team radiating brash power from every pore, evoking the universal essence of the jock. I never took the Beatles tour I wished to take; instead an Amy Winehouse mural in a market moved me to tears, along with the news that Dolores O'Riordan, lead singer of the Irish band The Cranberries, died in her hotel room at the London Hilton on Park Lane, right at the mid-point of my visit. When I travel, the beauty and the tragedy of life becomes heightened for me. I was struck by the thought of two brilliant singers, gone too soon.

* * *

I am excited when the day arrives for my visit to London's independent Feminist Library, but time is getting away from me. It is now late in the afternoon. The wind and rain are wicked as I ascend from the Elephant & Castle tube station. I intended to walk to the library, but the weather is brutal as I stand in the crosswalk with a crowd of people. A woman's umbrella flips inside out, and she shouts in a surprisingly Cockney accent, "The fucking thing has broke!"

The skies are darkening. I hail a taxi, the cabbie hesitant to drop me in the less traveled set of blocks near the rail yard. "Are you sure this is a library, Madam?" I see a man looking at the names next to the buzzers on a directory outside the building, and Feminist Library is one of the listings among other non-profits. Together, we are buzzed in, and the cab departs.

"Are you here for the party?" the man asks me. "No, I'm here for the Feminist Library," I say. "So am I!" he says, "My friend has booked the Feminist Library for her birthday party." The setting is unlikely. A non-descript building, with long hallways and partly abandoned offices. Up one floor, we are greeted by a bright-eyed, somewhat preoccupied woman in her thirties who directs the man to the very real birthday party upstairs, and me to roam the cramped but joyous stacks of the library. As I peer into its back office, I am surprised to see someone I recognize: an archivist from a library I visited the previous week. To be in a city of eight million and to connect unexpectedly with a familiar face is a gift. I am more at home now.

In its humble setting, London's Feminist Library is an extremely special place. The library has existed since 1975, always staffed by volunteers, a true collective. Books are shoe-horned onto shelves going in all kinds of directions, in a unique classification scheme that makes browsing easy.

As with any library there's a sense of stepping into the past, as the feeling immediately conjures for me four different milieus at once. First, the days-gone-by feminist bookstores, with the bulletin board of community events. I see many familiar imprints, books that defined a decade. Second, the various Women's Centers I've visited over the years, generally on college campuses. Third, the feminism section (the HQ 1100's) in the library I work at. Fourth, and most powerfully, the personal book collections of well-read feminists. Back in Seattle, I have visited the homes of women downsizing, wishing to donate their feminist collections to a library. Although I never enjoy telling them that their collections mostly duplicate what we already hold, today I'm looking at things differently. Redundancy is not always bad. So what if we all had a copy of *This Bridge Called My Back* or *Waiting to Exhale?* It's magical that Londoners have a place where these works can be held—yes, held in hand!—by today's and tomorrow's readers. For free. I pull a book off the shelf and it is by a Nova Scotian descended of Black Loyalists, the poet Maxine Tynes. I open randomly to her poem about a tragic event in Montreal, the École Polytechnique 1989 murder of fourteen female students, before we used the term "mass shooting" every few months.

The Feminist Library has a bookstore, my main purpose in visiting it. I am directed to a library book truck filled with items, alongside a table with sale books displayed on it. "This is our book shop," explains the woman, "and if you'll excuse me, I need to bring champagne upstairs for the party."

I peruse the "shop," checking materials against our library's online catalog using my cell phone. I'll purchase whatever looks good that we don't have. Luckily there's fertile ground here, especially the zines. As I go to pay for the materials, it's a mix of old and new technology. The young woman accepts my U.S. credit card payment via an adaptor snapped onto a mobile phone, but I need a full receipt, with each title listed. There's no way to type or print that makes sense, so she starts hand-writing out a list for me. It needs to be on letterhead, I tell her, which doesn't exist. We cut the Feminist Library logo off an envelope lying on the desk, and staple it to the "receipt," which the saleswoman signs. The revelers descend from upstairs.

The eight or so people want to walk around the library, and the American ex-pat whose birthday it is wants to tell us about the importance of the library. The group wants to know about me, and I explain my feminist and queer book-buying trip. They are departing to a live music venue. "I hear you're hitting a jazz club now," I say to the birthday woman.

"I love your American accent!" exclaims one of her friends. "*Hitting a jazz club!* – it sounds so good the way you say it." I laugh and recognize my unacknowledged privilege, how rarely it has been that someone has commented on my accent. After all, I say things "normally," right? But yet the woman with the broken umbrella had seemed hilarious to me. Only through getting outside my country of origin do I realize that I am an American. I sound like one, I must think like one. Unlearning some of this is my goal now, to make room for new understanding.

I do ruminate, post-travel. I use my commute time to make careful online photo albums, setting images to music, and I watch these homemade "movies" dozens of times. As I commodify my own nostalgia thanks to Apple software, I consider what is left out of my narratives. I go online to research places that hooked me. I learn that the Feminist Library successfully raised money to move to a much better location. For my 2018 memory montage, I choose images of the libraries, archives, museums and bookshops I visited, and snapshots from my private walks, unexpected sights like black swans or a "rough sleeper" in front of the St. Pancras Hotel. The musical selection was easy: it had to be "Linger" by The Cranberries, which Dolores O'Riordan said was about her first adolescent kiss, a sensation she could literally feel on her lips for days. I know what she means. Sensations stay with me too: the warm air as the train rushes by on the Tube platform, earnest handshakes from bookstore and library staff, soreness in my shoulders as I haul back to my hotel room a load of zines, comics, and books to pore over before packing them up to mail.

By the time I leave London for the last time, the service for Dolores O'Riordan has occurred.[6] They played live music at her funeral, as well as recordings: her duet of "Ave Maria" with Pavarotti, her heartbreaking ballad, "When You're Gone." Family and friends celebrated her life, then laid her to rest in her childhood home in Ireland, near the River Shannon, County Limerick.

---

6 "Dolores O'Riordan Funeral: Mourners Pay Tribute to Cranberries Singer," *The Guardian*, US Edition, January 23, 2018, https://www.theguardian.com/music/2018/jan/23/dolores-oriordan-funeral-mourners-pay-tribute-cranberries-singer.

Culture Shock: Traveling Beyond Memories

Sarah Rafael García

I landed at the Beijing International Airport late August 2004. As soon as I walked out from the baggage area, screaming taxi drivers pulled on my sleeves and wobbly luggage carrier. My two large bags and carry-on were overstuffed and challenging to roll on my own. I packed over ten pairs of shoes and countless brand-named outfits. A month later I learned most items would serve no use.

Before China, I assimilated into the "American Dream" and grew accustomed to personal drivers while on business trips. Naturally, I became nervous when I didn't see a driver waiting for me at the Beijing airport. As I pushed through the noisy crowd, Chinese men continued to pull at me from all directions. I sought signs in English, but everything was displayed in Chinese characters and pinyin.

"English? Do you speak English?"

"Yes, taxi-taxi?"

"How about you, do you speak English?"

"Hellooo! Taxi-taxi?"

"No taxi! I need to call someone!"

And just when I was about to cry, a young Chinese man wearing a cleaning vest signaled. Without thinking twice, I followed him—anything to avoid the mob of Chinese taxi drivers who reeked of cigarettes. The young man guided me to a pay phone and called my employer. We both waited smiling at one another for nearly an hour—while I imagined the worst. Eventually, my employer arrived, and we sped off into streets filled with bicycles, produce-carts pulled by donkeys, and chaotic traffic.

During the two months leading to my departure, I gathered all the legal documents needed and packed my bags with much attention, even though the actual decision to live in China was a quick reaction to life frustrations. Before China, I never stopped to think how I'd communicate with locals. I didn't even own a passport until I got one to teach English in Beijing but, for some reason, I was confident I could live in a foreign culture.

After China, I knew I didn't leave America to explore a new country. I ran away from all the expectations set by family, culture, and society. Yet, only forty minutes after stepping into the Beijing airport, I contemplated going back.

After I returned to the states, in conversation a friend said, "Have you noticed that since your eighteen months in China, references to your life either start with 'Before China' or 'After China'?" I hadn't noticed. But China had changed me: the way I dressed, my eating habits, the type of men I dated, how I pack for a trip, and even how I perceived myself and others.

At first, taxi drivers often said, "But you brown, hair no yellow," and "Maybe you Chinese." It took months, but I eventually found a way to explain myself.

"Wǒ měiguo rén, wǒ de māmā bàba mòxīgē rén"

"Oooh! American good, Moxige more good!"

It wasn't until I could say I was American, and my parents were Mexican, that Chinese taxi drivers accepted my physical features. In midst of explaining my appearance to a vendor at an open market, she said, "America rich, Moxige poor." She gave me a Chinese price on a knock-off handbag because she thought I was poor enough. In that moment I learned to use my Mexican identity as an advantage. Unlike my experiences in the U.S., in China I was empowered by my Mexican roots. I was also able to claim Mexican citizenship because of my mother's lack of citizenship in America. Not only did I register with the U.S. embassy, but also with the Mexican embassy. In return, I was offered special privileges as an honorary Mexican citizen. I was invited to sophisticated galas through the Mexican embassy and met numerous Latinx expats. In a sense, while in China I had more privileges as a Mexican citizen than I did as an American. And locals shared sincere interest in my family's culture as I did in theirs.

During a Chinese holiday-break, I accompanied my then boyfriend from West Virginia to Datong in Shanxi Province. We visited a hanging monastery, Yungang Grottoes, and one of the five great mountains of China—Héng Shān. Although all the sites were memorable, a local taxi driver taught me more about acceptance and Chinese loyalty than I could ever grasp from one place.

By the time we traveled to Datong, I knew how to negotiate with a taxi driver but to arrange for him to drive us for four days was beyond my level of Chinglish. Luckily, I was dating a man who spoke Mandarin and studied China's history. Between his charming jokes and cultural knowledge—and my eagerness to make our traveling easier than most days in China—we contracted a local taxi driver to drive us for four days. At first, I was skeptical about giving the driver half of the money upfront.

"What if he doesn't come back?"

"He's gonna come back. It's not like the states."

"But what if he doesn't, then we're out that money."

"He'll come back, if anything just to save face. Anyway, he probably needs the money to fill up his tank."

My boyfriend believed in what the Chinese culture promised. I was weary of everything. But to my surprise our driver was waiting for us when we walked out of our hotel the next morning. He waited while we hiked and visited sites. We treated him to a meal or snack along the way to reciprocate his loyalty. On the third day, the driver asked if we wanted to see the Great Wall. At first, we said no because we didn't want the added expense. We had both seen numerous parts of the Great Wall by then and I had my preferred location—Simatai.

But he insisted and we agreed just to honor his pride. All I understood was that we would visit one of the oldest parts of the Great Wall and his mother. On the way there we had to drive through a ravine normally life-threatening during the rainy season. Again, I found myself questioning the driver's intentions. I suggested turning back but my boyfriend just dismissed my concerns with a joke about being a stereotypical American.

Without much explanation, the driver made a few stops along the way to pick up groceries and a crate of beer. As we got farther away from town, the scenery became more rural and less crowded than the Beijing streets I now called home. From a distance the taxi driver pointed out the Great Wall. I couldn't see it. All I saw ahead was a dirt area with old clay towers.

"There! It's one of the oldest parts of the wall, he says."

"Are you sure? Those look like pueblo homes."

"That's what he said. Towers are used as animal shelters and some as homes."

"I thought it was the Great Wall of China?"

"He says, since it's so old, it's worn out by the weather and no one bothered to restore it since it isn't necessary."

"I'm not sure I believe it."

During my time in China, I visited eight different parts of the Great Wall, with eight additional trips in four different seasons to Simatai. One trip included a ten-mile hike from Jinshanling to Simatai with friends visiting from the states, another time I zip-lined over the frozen reservoir at Simatai because it was too cold to hike down the last mile—all trips required a ninety-minute drive out of Beijing. I also established my own tradition: I chanted my father's name at each climb to myself. But on my last day in Datong I was dealing with knee pain due to hiking Mt. Heng the prior day. So, I was happy site-seeing through a car window and humoring our taxi driver.

The rural neighborhood reminded me of my paternal great-grandfather's ranch in Matamoros, Tamaulipas, Mexico, which I got to see a few times in my childhood. This area of Shanxi Province was filled with sheep, horses, and goats. Each adobe house was adorned with a satellite dish. In some cases, the monstrous plate sat on a roof or near the front door with a cable leading inside the home. The driver's elderly mother greeted us while he carried in groceries and beer. She cooked for us while we went to see the nearby Great Wall.

Although the ruins could've been more impressive if I climbed an empty tower as both men did, I found myself content with limping around the dusty ground and thinking of my father who died before he could travel beyond the U.S. and Mexico. I chanted my father's name three times, once for each of his daughters, to claim the space as something we had done together. After all, because of him I aspired to travel and write and found the courage to live in another country.

Once we returned, the kitchen table was filled with a dozen Chinese dishes. The norm was one to two dishes per person, here we were only four and had a tableful, along with a crate of beer. I liked it all, but one dish reminded me of my grandmother's carne guisada. My boyfriend translated the compliment and the elder woman smiled and replied.

"What did she say?"

"Oh my god, it's too cute. She said, 'Tell her I'm her Chinese grandmother.'"

"Aww! Tell her, I'm her Mexican granddaughter."

And what she said next made the men burst into laughter. My boyfriend translated, "She said, 'No wonder you look Chinese not American!'"

The conversation led to a lot of back and forth translation in which the elderly woman admitted that we were her first foreign guests and inquired more about Mexican culture. Upon leaving, we captured the moment in a picture.

We had scheduled to take an overnight train to Beijing late in the evening. Although we were still full from lunch, we had to "save face" by obliging with the taxi driver's request to meet his wife and son over dinner. He refused to let us pay for any portion of the meal and countless amount of beer my boyfriend consumed. Although the train ride home was horrendous, given our tickets were first-come-first-serve seats on hard benches and the familiar face to my right was a belligerent American, it was then that I understood the Chinese culture to be very similar to my Mexican familia—hardworking, welcoming, and a full table surrounded by loved ones. I never doubted the working-class people of China again.

* * *

Going to China raised the same argument my mother and I had when I moved out of her home at eighteen. My mother didn't understand why I insisted on going against normal expectations. Before China, I crossed many types of borders with my family. Being the first-born in the U.S. and a woman came with many cultural expectations. I was expected to remain in my mother's home until I got married. I was expected to have my own family and still remain close in proximity to build a support system for my sisters and widowed mother. I lived accordingly for most of my twenties, putting myself through college, seeking a husband, and building a career.

By thirty, I doubted the gender roles imposed on me since my childhood. I couldn't accept the idea that my life didn't start until I acquired a husband or child. When I applied to teach English in China it was simply out of frustration and exhaustion. It was my way of telling everyone, "I quit this American dream!" But of course, I couldn't say that to my family. I presented my China escape as a sabbatical from my career to explore extended travel and writing. But my mother questioned all that led up to the experience.

"What do you mean you're going to China?"

"Why are you so angry? It's my life."

"But it's a communist country! It's dangerous!"

"Mom, it's not dangerous. I'll be fine."

"¿Como vas a sobrevivir allá? Do you even like Chinese men?"

"Oh my god, is that what this is about?"

"You're thirty, it's about time you think about it."

I can't say I didn't want a husband. I spent most of my twenties dating all kinds of men. The five years prior to my time in China I dated: a white man who had lived in Turkey and was financially supported by his mother, a Cypriot who hoped to become rich in America, and a rich Persian-Jewish man who broke off our engagement because his mother couldn't accept a Mexican-Catholic daughter-in-law.

When I first arrived in Beijing, mostly British and Australian men approached me. Maybe I was erotized or maybe I just caught their attention. However, in my situation men were more curious about my Mexican ethnicity than my American tendencies. Yet at the beginning, the American part of me surfaced into flirtatious conversations.

"So where are you from?"

"I'm from England."

"Well yes, but where are your parents from?"

"They are from England too."

"Seriously, are you Indian or Pakistani?"

"You must be American."

Not only did I realize how America's racial tensions affected my interactions with other people of color but also how naive I was about the world, especially when I was living up to the American stereotype. Although I never pursued anything with that particular British man, it was only a few days later that I met an Australian who was backpacking through Beijing en route home. He had just completed a stint as a traveling nurse in England and volunteering after the Tsunami in Thailand. My initial attraction to him was his accent and hero archetype. But after a few days of conversations and long nights of debauchery, I admired how easily he maneuvered through the streets of Beijing without a worry for tomorrow. Like me, he did not speak Mandarin or have much knowledge of Beijing life and unlike me he was only to remain in Beijing for two weeks. In the short amount of time we had together, I felt completely removed from the cultural expectations imposed in the U.S. and the worries of what might happen in the future.

Once I developed my own routine in Beijing, I began to miss regular companionship. When the young American from West Virginia first approached me, it was for a friendship. Being that he was five years younger and a fellow English teacher at work, I didn't consider him a potential partner. I had dated men a year or two younger than me in the states, but five years seemed like too much. But as we continued to enjoy each other's company over hikes, sightseeing, and drunken conversations in late night taxi rides our physical attraction to one another was inevitable. The first two months I was too embarrassed to admit I slept with a younger man, but eventually we dated openly for seven months. He impressed me daily with his ability to immerse in a different culture and also appreciate how mine differed from his. But unfortunately, my life in the U.S. kept interfering with my relationship in China.

"Ay Sarita, you went all the way to China to date a gringo from West Virginia? Are you two serious?"

"Ay mom, why does everything have to be serious? He's five years younger than me, we are not talking about being serious."

"Five years younger? He won't be ready to marry you, tú debes saber eso."

"Not everything is about marriage!"

My mother's reminders influenced how I dealt with the relationship. I found myself overbearing, judgmental, and unappreciative of what my boyfriend offered. I can say these things now because I have since married a Chicano nine years younger and I wouldn't be able to identify such traits without having my memories in China to revisit while redefining my female identity in marriage.

My time in China taught me to be less uptight and more vulnerable. Yet, it also showed different sides of me, a spontaneous and youthful side as well as a stubborn and traditional one. Unfortunately, my West Virginia boyfriend and I broke up due to respective personal issues that we weren't ready to deal with or commit to in a long-term relationship.

The break up prompted yet another persona. I was free to explore my sexuality, curiosity and true independence. While living in China I made out with a Spaniard, had sex with a Briton, explored vacation hookups with Greek and Turkish men while visiting Thailand, and of course there was the Australian at the beginning of my stay—all younger than me. But I only fell in love with one, the American from West Virginia. It wasn't until the end of my time in Beijing that I met an Australian from Canberra who engaged my emotions like the American. This time my partner was ten years younger and kept my attention for nearly three years after China. Like the first Australian, he too is now married with children. As for me, I have chosen not to have children.

Before China, I never thought I could live as I lived in Beijing—and be happy. Beijing was not a sabbatical and definitely more than an adventure filled with casual sex. My experiences in China sculpted who I've evolved to be since I left in March 2006. I learned to travel on my own as a Chicana, I learned to pack light, so light that I usually only carry two pairs of shoes and eight interchangeable clothing items in a backpack. I learned to appreciate my American citizenship and take pride in my Mexican culture. Before China, cultural expectations, material items, stereotypes, and gender roles limited me. After China, I changed the way I perceived my own identity and now live as a minimalist. Since then, I continue to explore, evolve and cross borders literally and figuratively, but now I know I'm not bound to live by any societal norms other than the ones I accept as my own. I learned to be me.

Rediscovering Myself on the California Roads
Valeria E. Molteni

This is the story of an immigrant, of a strong woman who felt lost after many departures in her life, a woman who had to redefine herself after becoming a mother. The journey which brought me to the United States started in an ocean city called Mar del Plata, Argentina, forty-five years ago. My voyage has been shaped throughout different hemispheres, countries, environments, languages, institutions, people, and cultures. My educational explorations have provided me different points of view that enriched my understanding of the world and defined my path as a librarian and as a feminist. I have been fortunate to study in three different countries: Argentina, Spain, and the USA.

My life navigations have been intense and rich in experiences; some full of happiness, some full of sadness. Travel for me is another way of learning through different lenses, and an opportunity to expose myself to the unknown to find my true self in the process. Immigrants are travelers who have the freedom to craft a new life in new shores, to change their cosmovision and beliefs, to choose to live in other spaces. I chose to speak a primary language different than my mother tongue, to be with a man from another continent, to live in another country different from the one where I grew up.

For more than ten years, my journey has been in California, where I built a home and a professional life from scratch. My last position in Argentina was director of a small library, but I had to start my professional career from an entry level position in my new land. Immigrants suffer a permanent sensation of feeling in the middle, of being in a continuous position at the crossroads. For many years, I have been holding my identity as

Argentinian, as Latino American, and as South American. Learning how to be an American citizen is a continuous juggling task. Becoming an immigrant helped me understand the eternal nostalgia in the tango music, a melody created by the immigrant amalgamation of the Buenos Aires immigrants in the 20th Century. Nostalgia is a bittersweet feeling, which grasps you in the most surprising moments, and it is a longing of better times, times that perhaps never really existed.

The beginning years of my motherhood were marked by huge personal and professional losses in my life. Throughout my life, I have experienced very irritating and primitive patriarchal behaviors. When I chose to be a mother, I experienced many impositions by society in general, as well as by people who should have been supporting me. I was surprised and hurt by judgments about my personal decision of being a full-time mother and professional. This situation made me feel even more lonely, far from my homeland and my long-time close friends.

Navigations are not always pleasant; you might encounter storms throughout your journey. The constant pressure of looking for success in my new land, a series of personal and deep losses (my father, a mentor, and my mother passed away in a period of four years) and the difficult process of embracing my identify as a mother put me in a space where I started to doubt my value as a woman and as a professional. These situations exacerbated my feeling of being far away from my destiny, from my shore, far from living a full and authentic life.

Two pilgrimages in the summers of 2016 and 2017 helped me find myself again and reconnect with my soul. These experiences were similar in many aspects, such as in the search for silence, in the serendipitous encounters of women who enlightened my path, in the driving of unknown long distances by myself through the magnificent summer Californian roads, in the exploration of my femininity.

The first journey was to the small city of Forestville in Sonoma County in August 2016. I did not have any specific plan; just enjoy my tiny cottage and the Russian River, explore some vineyards, and debrief from my intense learning experience of the Harvard Leadership Institute for Academic Librarians two weeks before. I enjoyed working with that group of people and being nurtured by their energy, but after such an intense experience I needed solitude and silence. I planned these travels because Sonoma County evoked peace in my soul through its endless gold roads. I had just packed some books and gotten ready to sleep and swim. I rented a tiny cottage for a few days, which was adjacent to a big house where the owner lived. There were days dedicated to the senses instead of abstract thinking, days of long walking, of smelling the vineyards, of seeing and feeling the California sun on my skin, of tasting the magic myriad sensations in the wine. Quite serendipitously, I ended up sharing the early evenings with the owner of the house.

These evenings were illuminated by long conversations about life with this generous woman, who helped me see my need to leave a place of work which had transformed into a space of toxicity for me. These conversations were profound, with a person who was generous enough to listen intently to my voice in the perfumed summer sunsets while we shared a glass of wine. Through these conversations, I started to feel that I could liberate myself from mandates anchored deep in my soul and I could choose where and with whom I work and how I experience my motherhood. Conversations about her experiences and losses, and how I have silenced my pain, woke my soul to how I could change my life and move away from spaces of pain. These conversations were the seed for a long period of questions and revisions regarding how I lived my life until then.

The second pilgrimage was part of a silent yoga retreat in the mountain area of Nevada City in July 2017. I was invited by a friend to this trip. My expectations were scarce. I was planning to enjoy driving up into the mountains, doing some yoga, and exposing myself to periods of silence. My generous friend helped to transform this trip into a real retreat for me. During these sunny summer days, she exposed me to the different artifacts to help to establish a vision and to unveil a path close to my soul. I practiced yoga and retreated in silent spaces during the mornings. I rediscovered the power of silence to quiet my mind and I started listening to my soul. I also met other women who valued the power of truth over pernicious environments. There was an element of authenticity in all the activities that I did during these days: the practice of yoga, meditations, the conversations, the quiet mornings, the sharing of the meals.

This voyage consolidated my decision of not working anymore in toxic spaces but also to explore how I would like to live the rest of my life as a woman, as a partner, and as a mother. I started reflecting on feminist leadership, and how I could embrace it in my next position. I contemplated the contrapositive of masculine leadership in librarianship. I was able to discern the reason why I was not enjoying my job anymore. I was feeling that I couldn't be a complete woman. I was not able to apply the nurturing skills developed during a long professional career in librarianship. I was not authentic as a leader, because I was not able to utilize all of my abilities. I had been suffering, because I had been impersonating a leader that was not true to my soul. After these days in the silence of the Nevada Mountains, I realized that I would be able to embrace my nurturing skills as a librarian and make an impact as a leader in other places. I would create a better life.

The experiences described above are things and views that others have discovered before me. As a woman and as an immigrant, I had the feeling that I couldn't stop and reflect. I believed taking the time to reflect was a luxury for people like me. Coming from a home and a life of restrictions, it was difficult to embrace the idea that I deserved a space of silence and contemplation. Social mandates indicate that you need to be with your nuclear family all the time, otherwise you are judged a selfish partner and mother. I still receive comments from many people about how often I go to conferences or why I decide to be away a couple of days out of my routine. After these journeys, I realized that you can be really free from social mandates. Crafting moments of silence are pivotal to connecting with myself, and I will continue to nurture them.

My journey is not finished, but now I know that I can choose how I will navigate my future destiny from spaces of light instead of obligations. These experiences gave me the freedom to choose how I want to live my motherhood and professional life and how to pursue this path. Today, I feel liberated from mandates and I feel full as a person. I am incorporating mindfulness in my daily activities, not only at my home but also at my professional practice. I am working surrounded by people that I respect and they value me on many levels. I am able to be true to myself and practice my profession from a feminist point of view. I have established a better relationship with my daughter and enjoy my role as a mother. The journey never ends, and storms may be ahead, but I can always take myself out on the road and drive beneath the impressively beautiful California sky to rediscover my soul again.

A Psychologist in Paris: On the Trail of Women Whose Ideas Changed the World

Sarah L. Hastings

Paul Simon's album, *Graceland*, hit the airwaves during my senior year in college, amassing critical praise for its original score and memorable lyrics. In the title track, Paul Simon sings, "For reasons I cannot explain, there's some part of me wants to see Graceland."[1] That line has resonated with me for years, because it captures the longing to visit a place associated with a figure whose influence shaped a person and whose legacy shaped a culture.

Paris has become my "Graceland" over the past several years. I wanted to walk where feminist philosopher, Simone de Beauvoir, lived and wrote. My years in college and my graduate training as a psychologist exposed me to none of de Beauvoir's writing. Paris, from my perspective at that earlier time, was the place Freud studied with Jean-Martin Charcot, observing his clinical demonstrations of hypnosis in 1885 and laying the foundation of his theory of psychoanalysis. Charcot's patients, women seeking help for a variety of internalizing symptoms, were often labeled as "hysterics," an obsolete, catch-all diagnosis colored by a misogynistic history. Paris is known, too, for its role in the early Moral Treatment movement, the gradual progression toward providing humane care to those struggling with mental illnesses. In a famous 1876 painting by Tony Robert-Fleury titled *Pinel Freeing the Insane*, French physician, Philippe Pinel is pictured removing the chains from a woman at Hospice de la Salpêtrière in the late 1700s. The image, included in many introductory psychology textbooks, signifies the importance of this shift in how we understand mental illness.

---

1   Paul Simon, "Graceland," 1985–1986, track 2 on *Graceland*, 1986, Vinyl LP.

Freud and Charcot were both men, of course, and as with much of the history handed down to us, including the history of my profession of psychology, men's lives are afforded center stage. Having studied feminist psychology more closely over the past several years, I found myself drawn repeatedly to de Beauvoir's work and curious as to who she was as a person. When a research abstract I had submitted to a psychology conference in Paris was accepted, I decided to make the trip to present my project and to bring along my two teens.

None of us had traveled to Europe before. My kids had never been outside of the U.S. at all, and it seemed like an opportunity we shouldn't miss. I wanted to walk along the streets of the Left Bank, the avant-garde neighborhood south of the Seine River that produced a bohemian community of writers, philosophers, and artists during the first half of the twentieth century. De Beauvoir lived there with her lifelong partner, philosopher Jean-Paul Sartre, maintaining an open relationship that was the subject of intrigue and scandal until his death in 1980. The Left Bank has been home to numerous other counter-culture figures, many of them internationally recognized writers and artists, including Colette, Edith Wharton, Ernest Hemingway, Pablo Picasso, F. Scott Fitzgerald, and James Baldwin.

My decision to travel to Paris felt like embarking on a personal pilgrimage as well. I have been a single parent for more than ten years, focused on maintaining the safety and well-being of my two kids, now nearly adults. As a parent, we do what we can to mitigate risk—to assure our children are safe, that our finances are in order, that there is a community that supports them, and that, when possible, some variation of a safety net is knit securely beneath it all. Traveling alone outside of the country with kids feels risky. What if we get separated? What if our passports are stolen? Now, with both of my children on the cusp of adulthood, I felt more confident bringing them along for the adventure.

As we anticipated the trip, I read more about de Beauvoir. She is best known for her 1949 two volume The Second Sex[2], an analysis of women's oppression. Her work paved the way for the second wave of feminism which emerged full force in the 1960s marked by calls for equal access to employment and reproductive healthcare and acknowledgment of violence against women. Her writing inspired American feminist author Betty

---

2   Simone de Beauvoir, *The Second Sex* (New York, NY: Alfred A. Knopf, 1949/2010).

Friedan to develop *The Feminine Mystique*, a work credited with ushering in the women's movement of the 1960s and 1970s in the United States. In writing "One is not born a woman but becomes one," de Beauvoir argued culture creates women, molding them to adhere to a role society expects them to play. De Beauvoir rejected notions of a "natural femininity," citing the many ways girls are socialized to become the women their particular culture requires. She explored the idea that throughout human history, women have been constructed as "the other" by men, who have placed masculine experiences and perspectives at the center of things. In an effort to excuse themselves from having to understand women, de Beauvoir hypothesized, men attributed an aura of mystery to women. Because women were so complex and confusing, men reasoned, they could not be understood even if one tried! Women have been portrayed as fickle, flighty, ruled by mysterious forces like intuition and hormones, and too unpredictable to be taken seriously. De Beauvoir extended her descriptions of the dynamics of power and oppression to other social hierarchies humans have erected across the ages, including race and class as examples.

Reading de Beauvoir's writing today, many people express surprise that her words generated so much controversy. Her ideas don't feel particularly revolutionary anymore. Even if the broader culture of the 21st century has not fully integrated them, her assertions are at least familiar to us. In 1949, however, French society was more conservative than it is today. De Beauvoir had dared to criticize French patriarchy. The Catholic Church, which wielded enormous power, banned the book. Because women in France only cast ballots beginning in 1945, their voices and opinions had gained little foothold in the political sphere. The fact that de Beauvoir's assertions barely raise eyebrows in our contemporary world speaks to her influence and to the power of her ideas to take root in the seventy years since she penned them.

As I was exploring ways to discover more about de Beauvoir in Paris, I learned of a walking tour titled "Women of Paris." The website said it offered a glimpse of lesser known aspects of the city's history, "One dominated not by great men but by inspirational women, who persevered within a bastion of patriarchy to make their mark on Paris, and the world."[3] Perfect! I secured tickets for our first full day there, anticipating the tour would include details about de Beauvoir's life. As it turned out, a two to three hour walking tour reviewing

---

3   Women of Paris Walking Tour, n.d., https://www.womenofparis.fr/.

nearly 2000 years of Parisian history is limited in the depth it can provide to the life of a single individual. De Beauvoir was included, along with historical figures across the entirety of Parisian history. Several were new to me.

Our guide's narrative began with Genevieve, the patron saint of Paris. Genevieve is credited with convincing terrified early Parisians to remain in the city as they anticipated an invasion by Attila's Huns in AD 451. She led a multi day prayer effort that was believed to have saved the city from the Huns who set their sights on the settlement of Orleans, ransacking it instead. Ten years later, Genevieve intervened again on behalf of Paris—this time with a Germanic invader so she could prevent weary Parisians from starving. Genevieve managed to feed her besieged city by crossing the battle lines in a small boat to retrieve grain, and she negotiated with the warriors to release their captured Parisian prisoners. Upon her death, Genevieve was interred within an abbey. Citizens paraded her relics through the city on a regular basis to ward off mass illnesses for centuries, prompting Louis XV to commission a larger church to house her remains. The French Revolution intervened, however, and most of Genevieve's remains were lost to history.

The guide's narrative continued with Marie Curie's life story. I was a bit embarrassed to admit I knew few details of Curie's life. Born in Poland, but later naturalized as a French citizen, Curie is recognized for her contributions in radioactivity. She was the first woman to win a Nobel Prize, and the first person of any gender to win two Nobel Prizes—in chemistry and physics.

As our walking tour continued through the Left Bank, and I imagined de Beauvoir's footsteps where I was now walking, we stopped at a small plaque marking the original location of Shakespeare and Company, a bookstore and lending library operated by Sylvia Beach from 1919 to 1941. Beach challenged social conventions of the day as a lesbian. An American expatriate, she assumed considerable financial risk agreeing to publish James Joyce's controversial work *Ulysses* when larger publishing houses rejected it. Her shop provided a social and intellectual gathering place for writers and thinkers of the interwar period including Ezra Pound, Ernest Hemingway, and Gertrude Stein. Beach suffered significant financial losses after Joyce eventually signed on with a larger publisher leaving Beach holding debt associated with the original publication of Ulysses. She closed her shop during the German occupation of Paris, was arrested, and held at an internment camp. After the war she published a memoir recounting the intellectual and cultural climate of Paris in the years between World War I and II.

Our tour ended on the small island in the middle of the Seine River, home of Notre Dame cathedral, and the site on which the settlement that was to become Paris originally was established. The river served as a natural moat surrounding the small tribe of Gauls who settled there—protecting their village which, in subsequent years, expanded outward to become the city today. Stone ruins remain from that time period. Facing downstream on the Seine, the Left Bank, appropriately named, is visible on the left side of the river. Notre Dame burned just two months after we left. I am grateful we were able to see it before the fire, and I am relieved the bulk of the structure was saved.

One piece of history that was not covered during our walking tour was a dark chapter of Paris' story following the Allied D-Day invasion. During this time, French women accused of consorting with the occupying German troops were beaten, stripped, paraded through streets, and subjected to having their heads shaved by groups of men executing vigilante justice. Before our trip, I read an article by Ann Mah[4] about this *épuration sauvage*, or the wild purge, after France was liberated. Mah observed that these women, like sexual slaves and "comfort women" assigned to male military personnel throughout the history of global conflict, were often single, vulnerable women who resorted to sleeping with German occupiers to overcome loneliness, bargain for protection, and secure food for their families. Mah was kind enough to reply to an email before my trip where I asked for her guidance in learning more about that time. She cautioned the topic is largely taboo today, writing, "…the war is still a sensitive topic in France, with much lingering regret and shame. The *épuration sauvage* is not generally a topic freely discussed, and I found many people remain closed to it…."[5]

I broached the topic privately with our guide, a university student from the U.K, once the tour was over. She concurred the subject remains a difficult one. The occupation, collaboration with the Nazis, the deportation of Jewish French citizens to concentration camps, all remain a source of enormous shame. Mah recommended Anne Sebba's *Les Parisiennes*[6], a book

---

4 Ann Mah, "This Picture Tells a Tragic Story of What Happened to Women after D-Day," *Time*, June 6, 2018, https://time.com/5303229/women-after-d-day/.

5 Ann Mah, email message to author, November 2, 2018.

6 Anne Sebba, *Les Parisiennes* (New York, NY: St. Martin's Press, 2016).

detailing the lives of women living in Paris under Nazi occupation. It provides spectacularly detailed stories of a diverse group of women, including those who collaborated and those who were part of the resistance.

Our remaining days in Paris provided opportunities to visit the essential sites—the Eiffel Tower, the Louvre—but we added some additional priorities to our list based upon my desire to pay homage to de Beauvoir, and locate sites connected to Freud and Pinel. Wandering through the shaded pathways of the Montparnasse Cemetery, we found the graves of de Beauvoir and Sartre, tucked together beneath the trees, their grave stones covered in red lipstick kisses left by visitors (fig. 1). My son helped us navigate the Paris Metro to find the stop closest to Petié-Salpêtrière Hospital, the location of Freud's early training in the late 1800s and the site of Pinel's revolutionary efforts to treat psychiatric patients more humanely. The hospital remains in service today, so we did not attempt to go inside. We did walk around the exterior to find a grand, though admittedly eerie, early entrance to the hospital likely dating to the 1600s (fig. 2). We searched for the statue honoring Pinel, and almost missed it due to the visual obstruction

of earth-moving equipment and orange netted construction fencing. I wondered if the monument had been removed in an effort to reconfigure the traffic pattern and grounds.

My son saw it first behind us, calling out above the din of construction, traffic, and trains, "Is that it?" Indeed, it was! Sculpted in bronze in 1879, an 18th century "Docteur Philippe Pinel" is portrayed in a bold heroic stance, holding a link of chain, a female patient sitting meekly at his feet (fig. 3). My 21st century eyes were a bit unnerved with the positioning. Clearly, Pinel's actions were significant and he should be remembered as a major figure in the evolution of humane psychiatric care. My discomfort looking up at his image reminded me that when we elevate a person—usually a male—as a savior, we diminish the status and contributions of those whose lives intersect with that "savior"— those who are depicted as needing to be rescued. The woman sitting at Pinel's feet is reduced to a

Figure 1

Figure 2   Figure 3

stereotype—a victim, indebted to the man who releases her chains. I found myself wondering "Who is this woman? What has she endured? What is HER story?"

This pilgrimage began with me wanting to roam the streets where a woman I admired, de Beauvoir, had walked and where she trusted in the value of her ideas enough to weather the onslaught of bitter criticism in her day. I learned about a new heroine, Sylvia Beach, who lived her life boldly and unapologetically, and I came to appreciate the contributions of one of the most important scientists of the 20th century.

When I began this project, I conceptualized a pilgrimage as a culmination—a grand journey executed after ample dreaming and planning. In hindsight, I think I imagined completing it would feel like having accomplished a task on one's bucket list. I always feel a bit of satisfaction checking items off a list in anticipation of taking on the next "big thing." This experience, however, was not that. It was more akin to unlocking a treasure box or opening a door that reveals a whole new world that we didn't know even existed. This pilgrimage presented me with a door behind which resided a wealth of stories that were new to me. I find myself longing to learn more about the people I met through this journey, and understand how their lived experiences dovetailed with the cultural milieu of their time to produce revolutionary change and sustaining contributions. I am reminded of Dorothy in the Wizard of Oz having survived the tornado, opening the door of her battered house to find a new land alive with color and sound. Visiting Paris was my door opened to a vibrant world full of new ideas and perspectives laid before me by women who lived in another time and place. This pilgrimage was a call—to discover new stories, to sit with complex truths, to know characters more deeply, and to understand life in an earlier time.

I once heard a metaphor (and have not been able to trace its source) that likens our lifetime to the experience of stepping into a room where a loud, crowded party is already in progress. People in that room are engaged in spirited conversations about the important issues of the day. Initially, we inch our way into that space, listening, watching, and absorbing all that others have to say. Once we have a feel for the topics of those conversations, we join in. It is awkward at first, but gradually, we find ourselves participating in and even shaping the conversation, all the while drifting, along with the crowd, toward the opposite door where we exit, our time at the party having come to an end. We only get to participate in the conversation taking place in that room during our lifetime. The trip to Paris, though, has gifted me with the sense that I've been able to at least *listen in* on the action happening there years before I even got close to the entry door.

The Mother Road

D. D. Wood

for Gina and Glynis

"Highway 66 is the main migrant road. ... 66 is the path of a people in flight. ... 66 is the mother road, the road of flight."[1]

John Steinbeck

She was iconic to me. The woman who had walked the "path less taken," a life that I had longed for but lost. I was the George Bailey of Long Beach, California. Living my own version of *It's a Wonderful Life*: Mother to all and yet always longing to be free for just a moment to see what a solitary life as an artist felt like.

I knew of Georgia O'Keeffe from my earliest memories. Her heart on display throughout our home. Her flinty face emblazoned on the coffee table book of her art. She was a constant in a home where women were not only hearth and home but stoic examples of feminism of the 1960s and 70s: You could do it all and *Goddamnit you would*. So, I grew up as most girls from that time—knowing all of the traditional skills of cooking, sewing, cleaning well—but also what were considered boy chores of that day: car maintenance, wood working, lawn care, and fist fighting if necessary. My father was a feminist in a sense. He took great pride in the fact that as a small girl I was as "strong" as a boy and could do anything that any boy

---

1   John Steinbeck, *The Grapes of Wrath* (New York, NY: Penguin Group, 1939/2006), 118.

could do. But, he was also a traditionalist in a sense that I was his beautiful and talented little girl. I lived between the world of men and women of that time and traveled fluidly between—comfortable in the dual definition of who I was to them.

I was fifty when I decided to take The Mother Road to Georgia O'Keeffe's home. The Mother Road. Steinbeck's words for Route 66. Beckoning to desperate migrants. Beckoning. Not much older than she was when she chose to leave the East Coast behind and take this same road to make the Southwest her permanent home.

Like me she had left a marriage. Not because of a lack of love, but because her love was too great. Artists marrying artists, I had learned, rarely boded well and she was quoted as saying everything she was, was because of him or despite him, words I had always attributed to my own marriage. My family and friends never quite comprehending that though together we could never find a common ground, apart he still held my heart.

I took the 66 down from Chicago. It began with a jump and a tap of my hand against the sign post on Adams and Wabash and not an easy jump and tap at that. It's a good, solid climb up to the top of a street pole and though I was fifty, quite chubby, and in a dress, I climbed it. It felt unlucky not to. It was as if that sign was a talisman for all travelers to have safe journeys on the road. I looked about a bit sheepishly as I began, glad for the early morning and that the local Panda Express was not yet open. Glad that people were not sitting at the counter eating their cream cheese rangoon and kung pao chicken while trying to ignore the middle-aged woman grunting up the light post. Or, maybe watching with amusement while sharing it on IG or snap chat hash tagged: *#kingkong #notbeforemycoffee*

I climbed and I struggled but made it up to barely tap the bottom of the sign where it says "begin" and so, out of breath and already sweaty, I got back into the car and hit the road.

The drive out of Chicago winds through the city, rolls into abandoned industrial warehouse shells, and then flows into long stretches of open road. A bit over two hours later I stopped for a moment to pray "*for a broken world*" as the sign states at the Route 66 Log Chapel in Lincoln, and wave at the world's largest covered wagon before driving on to Springfield to bow at the steps of Lincoln's home and quietly praise a beloved president—his vision for our country as vast as Georgia's canon of work and her painted New Mexico desert—then back to the road to greet the St. Louis Arch by noon.

90

Sitting outside what once was The Palace of Fine Arts, then The City Museum during Georgia's life and now the St. Louis Museum of Art during mine, I feel her siren song calling to me. *Dark Abstraction*, her painting now singing from the halls of its Midwestern home. Painted in '24'—dark folds of green and red—a fine seam of color riding between—like a road intersecting two worlds leading to a gray sunrise on a horizon. *Was this painting a premonition? Or a dream of what New Mexico could be? Was her new world already calling? Sure, that her husband's love affair would begin in '27.' An affair that would briefly crush her spirit but ultimately free her forever as an artist and a woman?*

I traveled on.

The long drive.

St. Louis to Oklahoma City. Riding Interstate 44. Watching 66 running beside me—weaving away but always returning as if to check how far I'd come and how far I would go.

Mid-summer and dusk arrived late. Now in Oklahoma and standing at the memorial I placed my hand on the second talisman of my journey: *The Survivor Tree.* 168 lost stood by me in spirit—lighting the way—reflecting in the water—forever in the stone as I silently watched the sun set and the sky grow dark. I was humbled by the presence of those we've loved and those we've lost before driving on to Amarillo—falling into the hotel bed exhausted—the hum of the road still vibrating through my bones.

Route 66 was barely three-years-old when in 1929 Georgia chose through heartbreak and physical exhaustion to leave her husband and escape to the Southwest and now 86 years later, I have followed her lead. I have found the light she left lit along the way—as bright as the morning sun—still bright enough to guide me as I turn towards Santa Fe. I look up as a photograph flashes in my mind: The Art Institute of Chicago— her painting *Sky Above Clouds IV*—myself standing in front of it and now I watch as the art plays out live in front of me in real time. The road opening up before me—the same sky she once painted above me—her stylized images of clouds taking shape extending out on an endless canvas of space.

I arrived at her home road worn—my hand-stitched floral dress damp from the heat—long hair wild, loose to my hips—braless and wishing to walk barefoot through her home. The women that ran the tour had family that once worked for her and the tours were now not only their livelihood but their history. They ran their fingers over the multicolored embroidery threads of my dress, stroked the long tendrils of my jet hair with their hands as if I had always been there: *like-knowing-like as we always do when we meet our kindred spirits.*

I had made the last tour with only minutes to spare and stepped into her garden, right before dusk, with the dry heat radiating across my bones and the hollow singing wind blowing across my face and through my hair.

I felt at home, as if my own great-grandmother were walking with me through the garden, so similar to Georgia's. I could envision Gram pointing out the hollyhocks or the wild flowers that had grown too unruly. Calling to me to taste the fresh lemon from the tree or exclaiming over the grand size of Georgia's beautiful blue agave.

And then, it seemed I was with my Gram's daughter—my grandmother—Gigi, as I walked into the inner courtyard, a courtyard O'Keeffe said had to be hers and felt the need to paint numerous times. My Gigi who loved her courtyard in her own isolated desert home of the high desert of California. Where she allowed me, as a small child, to roam freely through the wilderness for hours at a time. I spent those days collecting rocks across the sand or sitting on the stone wall looking out at the desert sunset, painting my own work of the desert sun, completely unfettered, joyous in my solitary ways.

I could see my own mother in the simplistic beauty of Georgia's home, in every ingredient that sat in open shelves in her kitchen, in Georgia's love of fresh vegetables and homemade pies and the plants that still sat upon the windowsill above the sink, long after her death. I imagined Georgia there, hands pressed gently on the porcelain of the sink, or mid-air posed with a soft towel over a warm, wet plate allowing her mind to roam over the distant mesa, free as she traveled through spirit. *Was she thinking of what she left behind? The child she always wanted but never had? Did she doubt? Did she regret?* And my own mother at her own kitchen window, where did her mind roam? *Did she lament marrying young? Was the love of my father strong enough to weather five unruly children, a house full of matted and muddy pets, a road not taken?*

The women of my youth were tied to her. Through tradition. Through home. Through me. Through love. The Mother of American Modernism like us caught between two worlds, learning to live fluidly between them, the artist that longed to be a mother of her own yet mother to an entire generation and to entire generations of artists to come.

And I know that *I am only a fragment of a whole. We are all only fragments of a whole.* And by journeying to be with her through the fragments of Route 66, through what America was and what America now is, I found that she is always with me and I am always with her and in my own life in Long Beach I too believe that there is something unexplored in women that only women can explore and so I will continue to travel my Mother Road, I will continue to dig deep, I will rush towards my own red rocks of salvation, I will leave my traditionalism behind but embrace it for what it made of me: *because and despite.*

Summer Lessons

Lucretia Tye Jasmine

Her yellow trunk sat, open, by her door. It was neatly packed. Some clothes still draped on her bed, falling out of her dresser's drawers. The casual lacings of Folly's white Puma tennis shoes made the shoes look ready to go as they waited by the corner of her trunk. I loved the single pink swoosh of a stripe on the sides of the shoes.

It was the late 1970s, it was the summer before sixth grade, and I lived in Louisville, Kentucky, a town too small for me. I was large, bigger than all my classmates and other kids my age. I'd been insulted for my weight by classmates, neighbors, and the first doctor I ever remember seeing, almost every year of my life.

In Folly's trunk were tiny t-shirts with cap sleeves, folded neatly and in pretty colors: princess pinks, mint greens, baby blues. Her open trunk reminded me of candy-coated Jordan almonds in a nifty box, what my mom always got at the movies.

Up to that summer after fifth grade, my mother chose all my clothes, and usually set them out for me. It made me feel safer, wearing clothes she chose. Elastic-waisted gauchos in earth tones. "So cute," she'd say. I'd struggle to agree. Mud brown, neon green, dead orange. Matching t-shirts. Where did she find them? Ugly clothes, unpopular girl clothes, uncool. "Adorable!" my mother would say, saboteur.

Folly had blonde hair and long legs. Her mother owned the house we rented. Folly and I were the same age. She lived downstairs with her mother and brother; I lived upstairs with my mother and brother. The house was a two-story duplex in a middle-class neighborhood of uniquely designed houses, each house different from the other, and my family had the side entrance. On the inside, a door at the bottom of our stairs connected our part of the house to theirs. It could've been fun.

Folly took ballet, her feet en pointe even at rest. Her smile as she played a bragging version of Show and Tell when we first met, explaining as she showed me around that everything they had was given to them for free by family: their groceries, their car, the house itself. Its high ceilings, all their rooms double the size of ours.

But I loved everything about the top floor we rented: my bedroom had a walk-in closet where I put my glamorous dressing table, the bathroom had a claw foot bathtub, and our tiny kitchen had a pantry. It also had a tall window which could open, and my mom would perch on its sill as she got stoned, staring out into the sky with her faraway eyes. Our huge stereo fit perfectly in the long hallway that connected the bedrooms. My bedroom had lots of windows, and in the wintertime, icicles seemed magical. That room was where I first began my creative writing. Folly sometimes watched me writing, her blonde hair on my pages as I wrote.

Folly's smile was a mean dare in cruel embouchure as she pointed out everything she had that I didn't, smiling as she pointed out her higher singing voice as she advised me: "You should just sing in a lower register." Mean-faced under her smiling as she noted her longer legs ("Like in *Cosmopolitan*."), her pale hair ("Do you think it's true blondes have more fun?"), her mother's long-term boyfriend ("Don't you think he looks just like Paul McCartney?"). My mother had temporary boyfriends.

That summer, Folly went off to camp. I looked at her yellow trunk, with all her pretty girl things in it. Neatly folded, her summer clothes looked like happy plans.

Her flat tummy flattered by all that she slid on (or off), her thin pale arms a perfect fit into everything she tried on. She had flowery camisoles with delicate straps. I'd never seen shirts like those, not for girls, just for women in magazines.

Her socks rolled, fluffy and absorbent, side by side in that trunk. Undershirts I wanted to mock. Her budding chest had pink nipples, secret girl peeking out. Tiny flowers. Her underwear was boring, plain and white. But she had shorts that zipped up the front and buttoned at the waist in many colors—Easter egg pastels, and all in comfortable cotton. I felt like an un-girl in my gauchos.

Her yellow trunk like sunshine for skinny girls leaping into tomorrow. Summer camp foreign to me. I'd never gone to camp. My mother's fear my own. Folly's mother went shopping with Folly at the mall, and they packed the trunk together. Had I ever been to the mall?

One time, stealing downstairs to steal some of Folly's things, I saw her mother cradling Folly by the fire. The TV was on. They couldn't see me as I peered through the slightly open door at the bottom of the stairs. The firelight – or was it the glow of the TV?–warmed their skins. Folly wept at her mother's breast, her feathered and shoulder-length blonde hair neat next to her mother's long, thick, and tumbling brunette locks. In my mind, they looked like a painting.

Mom said when she went to check out the duplex for the first time, she saw Folly bounding down the front steps of the big front porch, happy happy happy, thinking we were a visit from her father, the one who never visited. The look of disappointment on Folly's face stayed with my mother, whose ex-husband caused similar feelings of anguish in me, and my brother.

On Friday nights Folly and I played a board game that introduced us to art: pull a card, and guess the artist of the painting depicted on it. Michelangelo, Monet, Manet, Magritte—all the usual men, and all men, as usual. My favorite was Edward Hopper's stark art, with paintings like film stills. Sometimes Folly and I told each other scary stories instead. Folly knew all the scariest ones. Being around Folly was to be scared.

Her yellow trunk closed. She went away to summer camp. Her absence a relief. It felt like vacation to me. When she left, I felt like summer finally started.

That was when it occurred to me. I was thinking about The Fashion Shop. Their storefront featured romantic and playful styles I liked: seagreen sundresses, flowery hats, off-the-shoulder tops, and blue jeans. I had a bicycle I'd recently taught myself to ride after seeing Folly on hers. The Fashion Shop wasn't far. I could ride my bike there, I realized. I'd been saving change. I counted it up, and there was a lot. I could spend the money I'd saved on clothes I chose. I could try on the clothes, and buy them. I could do all that alone.

And so I did.

My body felt awkward and familiar on the bike, self-consciously not thin but sturdy and pliable with newfound determination as I gripped the handlebars, sat on the saddle, and put my feet on the pedals. My bicycle, a bronze-colored Schwinn ten-speed, felt open to my maneuverings. After an initial wobble, we rode unfalteringly down the street, over the hill and somewhat far away.

The air felt strange on my skin, like it was exploring me as much as I was exploring riding through it. My bike felt like it wanted to work with me. I really liked looking around at everything as I rode, too: other houses, leafy trees, the road ahead. The beige bakery, the grey grocery store, the orange mini-mart. And then, The Fashion Shop. It was in a strip mall, among a row of stores on a sidewalk amidst a parking lot. It looked poor in its cement and grit, tantalizing with cheap thrills and a smudgy pink sign. Like day-old dessert, it was good enough.

Opening the doors to the large store felt like bravery. Would I be kicked out for not belonging? But no-one gave me a second glance. It wasn't crowded in that silvery room. I looked at the other women, observing what they were doing. The women looked young, but not as young as I. They were all thin, and most were alone. They were standing variously and singly among the many circular dressing racks, simply combing through the clothing. So I did, too. A young woman near me, bare-armed and unsmiling, reassured me in her quiet self-involvement. She was looking for clothes. So there was nothing wrong with doing what I went there to do! And I wasn't being kicked out for being too young, too fat, on my own! Soon I forgot everything but the clothes I was choosing.

Shyly I stepped into the dressing room. Would someone halt me as I entered? I liked opening the curtain, movie-star blue and velvety. Feeling like a pretender to the throne, convinced the mirror would traumatize me, as it had so often in the past, especially when Folly and I stood together in it, I barely glanced at my reflection at first. I organized my clothing selections, soft material on my fingertips, and didn't look as I undressed and dressed, the project thankfully engaging me. But I had to look, ultimately.

The clothes didn't look that bad. I didn't look that bad! I looked better alone.

I bought: a light aqua wraparound skirt with fluttery trim, sky-blue shorts trimmed in satin, a halter top that seemed to flow with its light layers of semi-sheer flower print. A couple of very pretty short-sleeved tops in rainbow colors. One was excitingly sparkly!

The store clerk didn't even bat an eyelash when I set out all my coins in neat pillars to pay. She just counted it up. I loved how she folded my new clothes into a bag that had the name of the store on it: The Fashion Shop, with a flourish in the font. My bicycle was waiting outside, trusted friend. I tucked the bag in the basket attached to my bicycle's handlebars, and rode home like I'd been riding forever.

I listened to the radio a lot that summer, taping songs off the radio onto cassettes for mixtapes. I rode my bike to the record store, and bought vinyl records, 45's, 8-tracks. The first album I ever bought was Sweet's *Love is Like Oxygen*. When Folly returned home from camp, the energy of her experience vibrating on her skin, she played her time with her first boyfriend for me like a song, replaying it over and over as we analyzed it. Boys for girls a story that sustains, a song recorded once that can be played over and over, like memory. But I'd been listening to my own music. I didn't care about camp and I didn't care about her and I didn't care (much) about her new boyfriend. Her green eyes, her budding chest. Her undershirts. Her apple-shaped bottom that looked good in corduroy jeans, her pink nipples. Renoir once said he knew he had completed a painting when he felt like slapping the bottom of the woman in it. I didn't have a boyfriend, but I wasn't sure I wanted one. I wasn't surprised when her summer boyfriend stopped writing letters that winter, even though they'd kissed.

Something changed in me the summer after fifth grade. Maybe it was because I knew I was about to begin junior high school. Or maybe it was because I discovered the radio, current music that was popular, supplementing my adoration of music from my mom's generation and from my grandmom's generation.

Or maybe it was because I took a feminist pilgrimage. Riding my bicycle to choose and pay for my own clothes created a feminist self-reliance and discernment I've carried with me ever since. I could be how I wanted to be in the world. I discovered I could provide for myself what I wanted when other people could or would not. It's a life lesson that's important to me because I learned that I didn't need to rely on anyone else. I realized I could determine my course. I could be my own ally, I could be my own friend. And that's feminist.

On Bluebird Trail

Trysh Travis

In my Dallas, Texas, high school circa 1982, as in every U.S. high school then and now, there was a cluster of cool guys. Since I went to an arts school, hegemonic masculinity was inflected somewhat atypically: the alpha males were the graphic artist who already freelanced for the local paper, the sax player who blew the baddest-ass solo on "Birdland," the stage designer who got into Cooper Union, and so on. But inflections did not alter substance. This half dozen or so cool guys were fairly typical: mostly middle-class or above, mostly white, all straight, able-bodied, and good looking.

One of the boys—the most alpha of these alphas, really—had very progressive parents. They were Midwestern transplants and attended a church called "Unity" that advertised on the classical music radio station. They built a home computer out of a kit. They allowed kids to drink responsibly at their house rather than driving around getting into trouble, and they tolerated low-key marijuana use. In the backyard of their house on Bluebird Trail they had a hot tub that kids were allowed to use, but the rule was you had to go in naked because fibers from a bathing suit might clog the filter, which was very expensive to replace, considering the hot tub came from Norway.

My senior year I was pretty popular, and friendly with most of the alpha males. The summer after graduation, I dated the boy with progressive parents. On hot afternoons we'd drink brandy and soda and watch *Apocalypse Now* on the Betamax; nights we'd sit naked in the hot tub and talk about conceptual art. Sometimes, though not always, we'd have awkward sex. One afternoon in August my shift at the vegetarian restaurant ended early, and I prevailed on one of the cool guys who lived nearby to drive me over to my boyfriend's house. It wasn't hard, because he was going that way anyway—they were all hanging out for the evening. The parents were out of town.

The residential street was quiet when we arrived, but from the whole-house sound system strains of Jimi Hendrix drifted out to the side yard, just audible over the ceaseless droning of cicadas. I went through the gate and the friend who'd driven clicked it shut behind me. Four naked guys, my boyfriend among them, were in the hot tub. A case of Moosehead and a fifth of Jack Daniels were on ice nearby. Empties lined the edge of the deck. "Party time!" somebody said.

My boyfriend stood up, hip deep in the water, holding a beer. "Hey, come on in," he said, his free hand closing on mine. He looked me up and down and smiled. "You know the rules."

She who hesitates is lost—or, worse, she loses everything.

Without a word I stepped out of my Birkenstocks. I pulled my t-shirt over my head, eyes locked on the boys in the hot tub. I pushed my cutoffs down.

And by the time my bra came off, every boy had looked away. I twisted up my hair, slid out of the rest of my clothes, and climbed the redwood steps up to the hot tub's edge. After another wordless second, I stepped down into the burbling water. And as my body vanished, the alpha males gave a collective, inaudible sigh of relief. The auto-reverse on the cassette deck flipped the Hendrix mix to the B side, the Jack Daniels made its way around, and the afternoon passed innocuously. Two weeks later I left for college in New York.

* * *

Almost ten years passed before I thought again about that afternoon on Bluebird Trail. I broke up with that boyfriend midway through freshman year. A few years later, after moving back to Texas, I became lovers with one of the other cool guys—the friend who drove me—but he, too, hated Dallas, and we spent as little time there as possible during the decade or so of our on-again, off-again romance. It was the 80s, and I saw the men in my life just like the women: some were boring, some were jerks, others were wonderful mentors, lovers, companions.

It did not occur to me to wonder about that afternoon until I was a high school teacher. One of my tenth-grade girls left school mid-year, and, in a hushed conference, the schoolmarm-ish principal told her teachers that she'd gone to a party thrown by a boy (from another school, thankfully) whose parents were out of town. The only girl present, she'd played sex and drinking games with all the boys until she passed out. A cab brought her home as dawn was breaking; her clothes were crusted with semen and vomit. The school's official take on the event was a sort of sympathetic victim-blaming. The boys were the bad actors, but the girl was "unusually vulnerable:" she was from another country, and the child of a single parent. Her mother was a high-powered professional who left her alone a lot. The teachers' role in the situation was to quash any gossip we heard about the incident.

Breaking the principal's stern injunction, another young female teacher and I discussed the events at length. My colleague's sympathy was intense; she had experienced something similar when she was in high school. When I expressed surprise, she gave it right back to me: "don't tell me nothing like that's ever happened to you!" I wanted to treat the issue with the seriousness it deserved, so I thought hard.

I had a vague memory of the house on Bluebird Trail. There were some parallels—and, truth be told, I don't remember how I got home. It was not "*nothing* like that." But did that make it "*like* that"? Being sexually assaulted, I thought, would have left a strong impression. "No, nothing like that's ever happened to me," I told my friend. "I guess I'm just lucky."

* * *

Over the years the essential weirdness of that afternoon lingered in my mind. I held it up against the experiences of the other women—the many other women—I came to know who had experienced "things like that," and to the theories of trauma and recovery that I encountered as a feminist scholar of substance use and abuse. Other women's stories and feminist theory both offered a narrative that could organize the events of that day, but the fit between that template and my memory never seemed precise.

When #MeToo came around, creating, for the first time, a truly mass cultural reckoning with sexualized violence, I felt compelled to grapple with the persistent elusiveness of this episode, so I made a conscious decision to travel back to my memory of Bluebird Trail. What happened that day? Could I—should I—say #MeToo? And if I didn't, what should I—could I—say instead?

In my journal from the summer of 1982 I wrote a fair bit about that boyfriend, though not as much as I did about the boy who later became my lover. I hated my mother and could not wait to leave for college. I loved my mother and was sure I would never measure up to the glamour and intensity of New York City. If another waitress at the vegetarian restaurant would only go on vacation, I could pick up her shifts and thus earn enough money to buy less ugly snow boots, and my life would be vastly improved. I wrote nothing about the afternoon on Bluebird Trail.

After exhausting my basement archive, I sat and journaled again, free associating to call up the sense memory of the place. I remembered an adrenaline spike at seeing all those boys there in the hot tub, their bodies pale, hearing the gate latch click and wondering what was happening. I saw the condensation on the bottles of Moosehead, the guest bathrobes in a pile by the tub, half in a puddle, the cheerful red plaid darkening slowly to maroon. A pebble under my right foot as I kicked my Birkenstocks into the corner.

I remembered those things (and not much more) and I also was aware of them as the correct constituent parts of a survivor memory. Successive decades of feminist trauma theory, Lifetime TV movies, and student writing that tries to reckon with sexual violence—all these have instructed me in how to see what happened. Adolescent homosociality is enacted within (and constitutive of) patriarchal domination. When its toxic mixture of love and insecurity combines with alcohol-induced lowered inhibitions, the result is collective predatory behavior. The identity of the female victim—who she is, how she is generally perceived—is nearly incidental; what matters is that she can be used in the performance of masculinity for the other men in the group. Girls who derive their own status from the approbation of their male peers may say nothing about the event, reframe assault as consensual sex, or even repress the memory altogether in order to survive, or less dramatically, to continue benefitting from their proximity to power.

This politicized theory of sexual violence originated among cultural feminists in the 1980s.[1] By the mid-2010s it had become a matter of common sense, diffused from feminist organizations and Women's Studies

---

1   Alice Echols, "Cultural Feminism: Feminist Capitalism and the Anti-Pornography Movement," *Social Text* 7 (Spring-Summer 1983): 34–53.

classrooms like my own into the criminal justice and mental health systems. From there it was refracted first into self-help books and TV talk shows, then into zines, blogs, and tweets. It seemed to lose some nuance as it spread, but that was okay: I loved its sweeping fearlessness and demand for public reckonings. I loved its strength and sharpness, so different from my blurry memory. Teaching it was easy, the students' hands all waving for a chance to speak, their heads nodding in agreement.

But as I thought about my past with the roar of my students—and the twittersphere—in my ears, a tension between the personal and the political increasingly troubled me. Here were my messy, impressionistic, half-remembered details; here was an organizing schema that would bring them into focus. Was I scared on Bluebird Trail? Probably. Embarrassed? That would make sense. Angry? I should have been. Fidelity to what I remembered—and didn't—seemed a secondary concern.

* * *

Last summer I saw the man who was for many years my lover, who has remained a good, if geographically distant friend, and I asked him about that day. Perhaps unsurprisingly, he had no memory of it. He's the father of two teenage girls and, as I recounted the parts of the day I did remember, he grew increasingly uncomfortable. "There's no way what you're describing would have happened," he stated flatly. "Not any of those guys, and definitely not me."

But what is it I am describing?

Here is what happened: I went to my boyfriend's house; there were a bunch of naked guys in the hot tub. I got in too. We drank beer, shot the shit, and went home.

That version of "what happened" is factual but insufficient, failing to account for a strange energy that I distinctly recall but can't quite pin down. Of course, any mixed group nudity would have generated a "strange energy"—as artists, we prided ourselves on our bohemian values, but like most teenagers we were really quite conservative. I felt something beyond that—but *what* I felt is unclear.

So try again. A boy says, "Hey, our female friend is coming over, how about we freak her out by all being naked when she gets here?" There is general agreement that will be funny, and that the girl, known for her sense of humor, will also find it thus. The moment of funniness is the goal: transgressing social norms in the name of comedy. Set up tension, then release it. Repeat for as long as the beer holds out.

This is a plan for sexualized teasing that makes someone uncomfortable rather than for violence as such; for routinized, low-level meanness that doesn't even recognize itself as meanness, not for rape. Such "boys will be boys" pranking might have been excused with an eye roll back in the day. We know now, however, to place it on a "continuum of sexual violence" insofar as it can be experienced, in the moment or retrospectively, "as a threat, invasion or assault, that has the effect of hurting [a woman] or degrading her."[2] And we understand that, with the help of alcohol and (especially) the pornographic imaginary, such jackass behaviors all too easily escalate beyond the participants' intentions and control. But if we understand that now, does that mean it's what happened on Bluebird Trail?

My male friend's answer to that question was "no," and he justified it, unsurprisingly, via reference to his own character and that of the other boys. He knew himself, he knew his friends; they were not "any of those guys" who do things like think about raping women. His explanation begs the question of "who are *those* guys?" of course. But I think, on balance, it's correct. My friends were pranksters—good ones—and competitive, and they could be mean. That meanness was always gendered and often sexualized, and it was conditioned by their status in our school as high-achieving, attractive, popular boys. It would be easy—and not incorrect—to place their teasing on the continuum and watch it slide right over into the red. But such an assessment would fail to reckon with how much I liked it.

* * *

Around the same time I was serving tofu enchiladas and writing my college application essay, feminist literary critic Carolyn Heilbrun mourned the fact that "those women who have made their way successfully into the male-dominated worlds of business, the arts, or the professions have done so as honorary men, neither admiring nor bonding with other women

---

2   Liz Kelly, *Surviving Sexual Violence* (Cambridge, MA: Polity Press, 1988), 41.

[and] offering no encouragement to those who come after them."[3] I was one such honorary man, and though I resist the suggestion that the status is inherently misogynist, I admit that I made "[my] way in a male-dominated world...by identifying [myself] with male ideals and role models."[4]

I was at the house on Bluebird Trail because of that identification, welcome at an all-boys party not because I was the host's girlfriend but because my knowledge of *Monty Python* and *The Prisoner*—and my ability to drink beer—was unsurpassed. The scene that unfolded there, I realize now, cemented that status in crucial ways. For as I went back and aggregated the details of sun and cicadas, Hendrix and Moosehead, what precipitated out of the blur of memory most clearly was not fear or embarrassment (though I'm sure those were present) but the satisfaction that coursed through me when I stood on the edge of the hot tub and watched those silent boys look away from my naked body. That, too, was an adrenaline rush, greater than the one brought on by the click of the gate latch, and it came from pure joy that I'd beaten the cool boys at their own game.

My theories of gender politics were sketchy then, my feminism informed more by my mom's tattered copy of *Our Bodies, Ourselves* and the daily lunchroom struggle for visibility than by any intellectually coherent analysis. What I knew at the level of instinct was that those boys had numbers, they had size, and they had each other. I was alone, with nothing but the essential strangeness of my body to mobilize on my behalf. That and a decidedly unladylike rage to win. Whatever it was they wanted from me (and honestly, did they even know themselves?), I found a way to turn their desire back on them and make a space of freedom—however imperfect—for myself.

In hindsight, I see the costs that power—and the pleasures it offered—entailed. It's not the freedom I wish for my students, or my daughter. But it took me out of Texas, through New York and graduate school, and into a reasonably successful academic career. During that time I had more male than female mentors but, contrary to Heilbrun's account of the honorary man, I was not (I don't think) "remarkably unsupportive of other women, or unable to imagine other women as accomplished as [myself]".[5]

---

3   Carolyn Heilbrun, *Reinventing Womanhood* (New York, NY: WW Norton, 1979), 29–30.

4   Heilbrun, *Reinventing Womanhood*, 29–30.

5   Heilbrun, *Reinventing Womanhood*, 30.

I recognized that I had been raised by that rare thing, a feminist mother. I became a teacher in part to share that luxury with other women whose social locations had suggested to them that, unlike men, they deserved only limited space in the world. I considered that political work.

The outcry of #MeToo invited me to re-examine not just what happened on Bluebird Trail, but the feminist self that went into and came out of the events there. I had welcomed that popular discourse for the clarity and power I saw it bringing to my students, so I was surprised to feel it draining away both the specificity of my experiences and my sense of agency. What remained was a mandate to identify, to connect a lot of diffuse dots in very specific ways, and to resolve a gray picture from the past into today's sharp blacks and whites.

Such a resolution is certainly possible, provided I ignore the specifics of my history. Yes, I can see my friends' behavior on the continuum of sexual violence, not in itself a threat to me, but adjacent to, and in many ways preparing for, perhaps suborning, such a threat. I knew their meanness. But I also knew its limits, the vulnerabilities that accompanied it, the confusions they half shared with me on summer nights like that one. They were hegemonic masculinity, for sure, but they were also individuals, and their specificity resisted assimilation into today's tidy and teachable construct.

And when I turned the lens upon myself? From empowered social justice warriors on Facebook I learned not only that the events on Bluebird Trail were "rapey," but that they had remained marginal and half-remembered because of my "repression." My sense of myself as lucky became "minimizing." That I saw and raised my male friends' prank with my own sexualized show of force demonstrated my inappropriate identification with the patriarchy. Instead of signifying my youthful resourcefulness, calling their bluff evidenced (probably) my straight white privilege, and (definitely) my internalized oppression. All that was feminist melted into toxin: I sat alone in my basement surrounded by old spiral notebooks, my social network glowing angry and white.

* * *

In her classic study of *Surviving Sexual Violence*, Liz Kelley argues that "having no words with which to name and, therefore, understand experiences may result in the memory being suppressed."[6] I used #MeToo to go back in time because I thought a contemporary lens would help bring into focus a sexualized puzzle from my past and give me words to name and understand it. I got clarity, certainly, but of the unanticipated, funhouse mirror variety. My past remained a foreign country; my present—or at least, the hashtag feminist present through which I travel as a professor of Women's Studies—was revealed as equally alien.

So try this last, deliberately undertheorized, highly individual version: One day when I was young, I went to my boyfriend's house on Bluebird Trail. A bunch of boys were naked and there was a weird vibe. Maybe I was afraid, but since I didn't know any better, I acted like I wasn't. The foolishness stopped; I'm not sure why. In fact, I've never really understood what happened that day.

But you know what's funny? Nobody else knows either.

---

6   Liz Kelly, *Surviving Sexual Violence*, 144.

On the Road Again

Nina Clements

In October 2015, I left behind both my husband and my lover and drove across the country to California with my old friend Jake and my two cats. We drove from Center City, Philadelphia, and we stopped in Ohio, Missouri, New Mexico, and Arizona before arriving in Southern California. I was in search of the fabled clean slate, the fresh start, and I left everyone I knew behind to get it. At the time, this journey didn't feel particularly feminist, or any more feminist than usual, but I realized later that my need for independence was largely the result of my feminism, my belief that I could do everything I needed to do with the help of loving friends.

I never intended to have a husband and a lover—one seemed quite enough—but life surprised me. In the winter of 2014/2015, my marriage started to unravel, and I began to unravel along with it. My husband Jeff and I had been married nearly five years, together for nine, and it was time to have children. I had agreed to it before we married, had promised that it was something we would do. Something I would do, but I could not do it. Everything started to disintegrate, to break down. I could only sit and stare at a television, or my phone. I could not go to work. I could not speak. I could not make dinner. My psychiatrist called it a mental breakdown. Jeff rightly worried that it was related to our plans to have children. I didn't want children on a visceral level, even as I made pro and con lists and concept maps. My body was the ultimate decider. And then I did something that made it impossible. We were in couples' therapy one week talking about all the reasons to have children, and by the next session, I'd taken a lover.

But before that happened, I slowly emerged from the abyss of depression thanks in large part to a new combination of medications, a cocktail of antidepressants and a mood stabilizer, and even more therapy. I returned to the library where I worked, to being a reference librarian and standing behind the circulation desk handing out the dry erase markers to grateful students. The circulation desk was also in front of the reserve shelf. I noticed that one of my acquaintances, a philosophy professor, David, was teaching a Philosophy of Literature class, and that there were interesting books on the reserve shelf. Those books led me to email him and tell him how exciting I thought his class must be. I don't remember the titles anymore, but I must have thought they were really something. That email led to an invitation to guest lecture in the class, which meant a lunch get-together at the rustic Italian place down the road from campus. In our dark corner, I somehow conveyed my dissatisfaction with my marriage, but I don't remember what I said. Something negative and awful and probably undeserved. Jeff had patiently cared for me during my breakdown: he drove me to therapy sessions; he made all of our food and cleaned up after me. All those tissues in the bathroom, long hair in the drain. He also took care of our five cats. We had too many cats, but that was the least of it. That lunch was just the beginning. David later told me that I'd given him a clue.

Soon, we were going to the movies together and meeting for dinner. David even invited me to his house in West Philadelphia, but nothing inappropriate happened. His house was magical in that it was old and full of plants with incense sticking out of them and more books than I'd ever seen outside a bookstore or library. Every room in the house was lined with bookcases, even the bathroom (Herodotus and other ancient texts). I'd come to think about all that Herodotus later, how full of lies it was.

There was, of course, a tipping point. He became my lover somehow, one night, in the back terrace of an Ethiopian restaurant, over countless glasses of red wine. He asked me to kiss him, and I must have done so. It's so blurry and wine-laden now. I remember the chairs were uncomfortable, but I don't remember what they looked like. I remember his fingers crawling over my rings, my amber ring from Colorado, even my wedding ring, like ants. Somehow, after nine years of only kissing Jeff, I was kissing David. It felt so overwhelmingly different, like I was a different person entirely as well.

And the one thing led to another thing, a more irrevocable thing. I'd had too much to drink to drive back home to Jeff, so I called him and told him I was staying over at David's place. He did not object, which I didn't think about until long after. I came to think later that we shared some responsibility for what came next. He had predicted that David was "after" me, but I was too depressed to believe that anyone would want me, let alone pursue me. As usual, I lacked perspective.

When I got home the next day, after brunch with David, where he read me Bukowski, I told Jeff about the kissing, which was not all that I remember happening, but it was the part of the truth I was able to share. He was very calm and very angry. He took off for a few hours to a coffee shop to think and work. We didn't argue. When he got back, we talked about finally opening up our marriage, something that he had wanted to do for a while. This time, I agreed. And so it was that Jeff and I became roommates who still occasionally showered together but never touched.

Jeff and I went on vacation that summer, to the beach in Maryland, to decide whether or not to stay together or to break further apart. I was also preparing for a job interview out in California. It seemed like a good idea to get on the other side of the country from everyone I knew. I wanted a new beginning, to be in a place where my favorite cat hadn't died from cancer, a place where I hadn't promised to do the impossible. During our vacation, David texted constantly. He did not like that I was on vacation with my husband. He was surprisingly possessive and intense, though I don't believe he liked me very much; I think he liked the idea of me. I'd never really cared for the words "husband" or "wife" or the ownership of another person they implied. I always referred to Jeff as "that fellow I married." I suppose that's what you'd call *telling*.

Somehow, I got that job at a college library in California. When I told David I was leaving, he grew angry with me. I suppose he wasn't used to being left behind. He said he thought I'd be more thoughtful about the decision, said that I was giving up on our university without giving it a chance. Jeff, though, understood my need for a new beginning. I existed with conflicting ideas in my head: I thought that David and I could still be together once I was out in California. I didn't want to stay in Philadelphia. The key was for David to visit me at Thanksgiving.

I marked the occasion of my journey by tattooing myself from wrist to elbow, a centuries-old phrase of the anchorite and mystic Julian of Norwich I was repeating to myself over and over again: *All shall be well, and all shall be well, and all manner of thing shall be well.* I was writing it over and over again in my journal, saying it to myself like a mantra.

I did not ask David to drive to California with me, and I'm glad of that now. Instead, my friend Jake took the bus from New York to Philadelphia, and we met on the street near Jeff's new apartment, where we slept with the cats that last night before driving off to our first stop, Ohio, the next day. Jeff and I were down to four cats. We would each have just two, which seemed strange and not enough.

It was like old times, Jake sweeping in to pick me up from the floor, or to prevent me from landing there in the first place. We went together to give Jeff the keys at his work. He kissed me on the cheek through the open car window, and it felt like the last time I would ever see him, ever kiss him. It wasn't. Jake was there with me, a witness, and though my eyes filled with tears, I did not cry. It didn't feel real but it felt right. In the car we had packed the cats, the Vitamix, the tea kettle and tea, and a few changes of clothing. I think there may have been a bottle of Maker's Mark for emergencies. I brought knitting for passenger time. My cat Maisie meowed the entire time.

"You've got something on your arm," Jake told me and laughed. He did this a few times on the journey. First, we drove to my friend Carolin's house in Ohio, a glass box on the river, so beautiful. We brought the cats out of the car to discover that Diablo Kitty, the baby of the family, had peed in his carrier. The cat and I went into the shower, a stream of sulfur water, and then we sat down to dinner. I'd lived near Carolin for five years while I'd worked at Kenyon College. Other friends from Kenyon joined us for dinner, and we passed a merry October evening. It was a gift to see them— it felt both surreal and hyperreal at the same time. It was full-on fall in the Midwest, the gray skies, the rain, the wind and the leaves. That's the last fall I've really seen, the last bare trees.

The next morning, we were off to Missouri. Diablo Kitty still smelled like pee. We ended up in a Motel 6 (pet friendly) that I wrote in my journal had "meth potential." We stuck out among the clientele, though they were white, too. We did not belong there, but there we were. A guy knocked on our door, but paled at Jake's 6'4" "Hello." I made him promise not to open the door again.

The drive through New Mexico was the most beautiful leg of the journey—the dirt was red, the sky was blue, and the mountains! The sky somehow filled the entire car while Jake drove and I knit. My college friend Ryan put us up at his apartment in Los Alamos where he and Jake talked into the night about nuclear stewardship while I went upstairs to sleep on the camping mattress pad with the cats. In the morning we went for breakfast burritos with freshly roasted chiles, green and red. Everything was so bright—I was glad that I'd finally purchased prescription sunglasses for California. I needed them. I told myself, this is your new life: *sunlight.* And it would be—I felt free and light, no Jeff, no David, just me and my friends. Soon, I would be free. It would be just me, and the cats in a tiny studio apartment I'd never laid eyes on. Soon, I'd be alone in a new town, in a new state, in a tiny space. But I knew I could do it. I was eager for the silence, eager to get David out of my head. We spoke on the journey, but we argued. He was or was not coming for Thanksgiving, he wouldn't commit, couldn't commit. The conversations we had were all brief and unsatisfying. The disconnection was real.

Jake and I stayed in the town of Williams, Arizona, near the Grand Canyon at another pet friendly Motel 6. We were tired and excited about the Grand Canyon, so we ate fried food and drank beer. We were eager to see the Grand Canyon but arrived too late in the day to make it out there before the sun set. We drove out to the canyon the next morning and took the cats with us. We left them in the car with the windows cracked for an hour while we gawked into the abyss.

When we got to the Grand Canyon and peered down into it, I was afraid of falling. There was only a railing at the edge of the cream-colored rock. The precipice seemed too precarious; I was afraid I was going to drop my phone, and there were all these signs warning you not to toss debris into the canyon; garbage was killing the already endangered California condor, one of the rarest of rare birds. We didn't see any of the actual birds, but the signs were plentiful. I felt deep down that I would be one of the people to bring them harm, that through my carelessness, I would take out a bird, so I gripped my phone tightly as I took photos and trod carefully on the rock.

Someone took our photograph, just once. Jake and I against the railing—you can see in the photo how tightly I've gripped it, slightly behind me. My smile seems small and strained against the canyon, but Jake looks happy, hands resting lightly on the railing behind him, one leg crossed over the other (fig. 1). Just a couple of tourists, for a moment. Not a woman leaving her husband and her lover for a job and a fresh start in California, not at all. This was the up and down of the journey, the back and forth between certainty and uncertainty.

We arrived at my new home, an entirely wood-paneled studio in Claremont, in enough time to lock the cats in the bathroom with their litter box before driving into LA to see the Dodgers play the Mets in the postseason. It was my first beer in California, and it felt wild of us somehow, as

Figure 1

though we snuck into that playoff game. There we were in Dodger stadium, when we'd been at the Grand Canyon that morning. This was my new life. We slept for the last night on the floor of my new and very empty apartment; I gave Jake the camping mat and slept on my yoga mat. I talked to David on the phone. We were still talking about Thanksgiving. I wanted to lock it down, lock him into place in my life as a visitor, as someone who still had a presence. But he would not be locked into anything. He wanted to hear about the Dodgers game instead.

Before I drove Jake to the airport, I waited for the dread to set in, to overwhelm me, but it didn't. I wrote in my journal, "All this here. All this emptiness. Emotional freedom." I drove Jake to the airport; it's the last time we saw each other in person. "Thank you," I told him and meant it. "This is it," he said and smiled. The car had started out in Pennsylvania and now it was in California. I was in California, ready to begin again. It felt like I had crossed the country on our journey, that I was somehow changed for it, even though so much of it felt blank and unknowable. It was a journey across the country, a journey into myself, and these men had helped shape that path. I was grateful to all of them.

Of course, it wasn't that easy. The movers came and filled the studio apartment. My entire life, all my books and journals and furniture, crammed into 300 square feet. I didn't have a mattress, so I slept on the green couch for the first month. My depression didn't stay behind in Pennsylvania, didn't hide from the sunlight. I would only land in that studio for a year and a half before I was onto the next beginning, but I was on my own, with the help of others. I lived alone, but I was not alone, not completely.

It was impossible to find the blank slate—I was still me, and I was still depressed—but the new beginning helped me. I wrote my way out of sadness in that tiny studio, wrote poem after poem for the first time in years, all while sitting at the red table, the same table I wrote at when I lived alone in Ohio. I faced my sadness with the help of my friends—old and new.

David did not come for Thanksgiving, even though he purchased a ticket. We would not have been kind to each other, were not kind to each other in the weeks leading up to Thanksgiving. Jeff came to visit that spring, though. We went out to Joshua Tree and hiked together. I did most of the driving, which was unusual. I was taking the lead.

A Heart Cut Out

Leah Jane Oliver

for E.

i

My niece and I stay up late, our toes touching on the blue velvet couch, a veil of trust settling over us through the wine and the hushed night. Everyone has gone to bed, and we light candles and drink more wine. She asks me how I discovered that I like girls. I tell her about Wolfsong, who was intoxicating in every way. Her leather jacket so small it barely reached her ass. She wore her hair short, with one black curl framing her forehead and wrote beautiful letters.

My niece tells me that my father, her grandfather, touched her when she was younger, that he came into her room when she was sleeping. She says it in anguish and disbelief. Later, I would be dismayed that we were drinking when she revealed this to me. That lack of clarity from the haze of alcohol would prove to be haunting, like a layer of gauze over an old photograph, hiding details of the truth. Her legs are long and take up the whole couch. I tuck my toes underneath hers on the far end. I tell her I don't believe her and then quickly take it back, gathering her into my arms. She is unwieldy, drunk, her limbs too long for me to fold in.

Recently, I've been reading everything I can on Elizabeth Bishop, the poet. In one article, the author uses the phrase "inadequate mothering" to explain why Bishop might have become alcoholic,[1] and in this moment

---

1   Brett C. Millier, "The Prodigal: Elizabeth Bishop and Alcohol," *Contemporary Literature* 39, no. 1 (1998): 54–76. https://doi.org/10.2307/1208921.

with my niece, I know my efforts are not enough, damaging even, and *I am not her mother.*

ii

One year later, I drive my parents to the Cape. I bring along a copy of *Elizabeth Bishop: A Miracle for Breakfast* by Megan Marshall.[2] It has already captivated me and I think it would make a good companion in our two-bed motel room. I want to discover why Bishop drank. It is said that at times she resorted to drinking perfume.

My parents talked about this being the last time. The last days to spend in a place fixed in my childhood memory, a place we have ritualized to the point of intractability. We plan our days around where we would like to eat, as if the staff are waiting just for us. My father has a peculiar way of toying with the menu, feigning interest in various dishes and then ordering the exact same meal each time: seared scallops and a Rob Roy.

The trip itself is pleasant, familiar. I remind them that we could just as easily return the following year. That this doesn't have to be the last time. This is more reassurance for me than for them, as it bothers me to think about them doing a last *anything.*

A recurring memory. It floats before my eyes like a movie still. My mother sits in the center of a two-seat wooden swing at the corner of the sun-washed motel building, her bare feet dangling above a dry patch of grass, her pink seersucker nightgown floating on the breeze. I'm not sure if this happened. My mother out of doors with just a nightie on? I have a whole series of photographs that suggest that it did, but I still doubt. There she is in my mind's eye, girlish and happy. My niece was with us on that trip. It was right before she went to college. She is the darling, coveted, youngest niece, a bit difficult to get to know. You get the feeling that she is calculating what it is you want her to say. You get the feeling that she is lying.

That was the year we got in a car accident on Route 6. My niece and I were together in the back seat. We are twisted, laughing, turning into each other. The sound of the impact is blunt and we stop instantly, air bags

---

2   Megan Marshall, *Elizabeth Bishop: A Miracle for Breakfast* (Boston, MA: Houghton Mifflin Harcourt, 2017).

pressing us into place like cookie dough. Later, I imagine my father looking at us in the rearview mirror, our laughing faces in view, a momentary distraction. After a few minutes, we stand in the hot sun at the side of the road, waiting for what comes next.

Elizabeth Bishop: lesbian, poet, alcoholic. How she would have hated those simplistic identifications. Yet, they made her like kin to me. It pained me to learn that she took Antabuse on and off during the majority of her adult years. The idea of taking something that you knew would make you violently ill if you drank strikes me as abominable. Especially when you consider what we assume must be truth: she kept drinking throughout it all.

The first night in the Cape Cod motel, my father overdoes it with the booze and ends up puking his guts out in the tiny bathroom with its scratchy white towels and tiny white soaps. Thankfully, the bathroom has a window to crank open in the aftermath. I put a cold wet towel on his neck.

Afterwards, my father comes out on the deck. We are quiet. I am unable to speak. The unspeakable! I knew then that it would be impossible to turn my father away. If I turn him away, I revile myself; I am lost.

I see how dependent my parents are on each other, a pretense, consulting each other on bizarre details like what shirt of the many identical shirts would be the right one to wear to breakfast. Does it have a stain? The vulnerability that they reveal is new to me, more childlike as they age.

The next night, we visit with old friends who have a cottage. It is festive and the two couples are conspiratorial. These are people I have never liked, but for no particular reason. The man flirts with me as if I were a 13-year-old girl come to sit on his lap. His wife swats at him and serves up overcooked noodles. On the way home, it is dark and windy and my father rolls the window down in the back seat. I chastise him because of the wind sucking through the car, though I know he is probably car sick from the bourbon rolling around in his guts. He struggles to get his seat belt on. He says wicked, barbed things, helpless. A giant baby strapped in, hurtling through space.

Suddenly, in the space of the car, I am enraged.

Cars are the perfect container. Sitting next to someone but not talking, wanting to get out, wanting to slam the door, wanting to change the radio station. A common trope in films, to use the space of a car to convey tension. You're sublimely trapped. You could die in there, sitting next to someone you can't or don't want to stand anymore.

At Christmas, I had confronted my father about my niece and he denied everything, anything, flung it all back at me. What I remember is the place, the driveway, being cold, with my arms folded over my chest, but lit from within, a fiery ball of rage fueled by hard liquor and the familiar. That was when I was still drinking. Anger, seemingly uncomplicated, the most facile emotion, a state of obfuscation. Anger is not: you failed me. Anger is not: I trusted you and now I can no longer trust anyone. Anger is not: you ruined my life. Anger is a blank. It had never occurred to me that he might deny this truth, that he might lie. It unhinges me and my heart falls out, not in neat cut out shapes, but in severed clumps.

In a film on Elizabeth Bishop, *Welcome to This House*, it is said: "She was a poet, a very good one, but she was a person, not a very good one. You have to live with that."[3]

iii

Just before our Cape trip, my mother received a letter. It revealed that something happened between my father and my niece and that he is an abomination and there will be no further contact with him. There are no details offered, no framing, and my mother hounds me to tell her anything I know. By this time, my niece has stopped speaking to me, maybe to anyone. I keep silent, wanting to protect my mother, but nothing I do or don't do will be right. I refuse to tell my mother anything; I beg her not to ask.

It is not my place. It is not my truth.

From that day forward, my mother sleeps in the twin bed next to me whenever I visit. Ostensibly, because a bat was flying around in the other bedroom. It is her primal response to the unspeakable thing. She is a bird sitting on her nest. Both eyes open. One night, we are up late. My mother tells a story of my father's father coming to visit her in her cabin at camp. She says he came to relieve himself (she does not use the word *sexually*). He was the director of the camp and she was working there over the summer. She refuses him and has him reassigned, away from the campers. She marries his son. My mother is the child of an alcoholic. She is steely. Yet, it seems unfathomable that she knew what to do in this situation.

---

3   Carmen L. Oliveira, *Welcome to This House*, directed by Barbara Hammer (New York: Barbara Hammer, 2015), DVD.

I turn this line of Bishop's over repeatedly: *so hot the blood in those webbed feet.*[4] It is stunning to me how lesbian this line is, it has an overpowering lesbian effect that makes the pulse quicken.

My mother has stories of me wandering away as a little girl. She says that I was picked up by a trucker once—that I had wandered far away from our campsite to the edges of a deep lake. Where was I going? I see my youngest self of memory or photograph, in a corduroy jumpsuit or pink toddler bikini, white zigzag trim, rickrack. It was all too much, even then, the responsibility of being with them. I finish the poem I am working on. Sometimes, when I walk through the pine beds and in the cover of trees, I know where I was going and I want to lie down.

iv

Having done with our beach vacation, we make our way to Connecticut to visit family. I walk the Quinnipiac River, amidst a forest of tall trees. There is a stone maze there. There are brutalist cement benches lining the path. They are sleeping places for giants. I write poems in my head. My mother is very quiet. Her sister knows something is wrong, but she has problems of her own. She tells me that she is taking Vicodin, I think, or Percocet. She breathes in short bursts and puffs the air out audibly. On the way home, I notice my mother is doing this too, suddenly holding her chest and blowing the air out through her mouth in a *woo- hoo- hee- hee-* pattern. It's annoying, as if she's pantomiming being an overweight chain smoker or actually having a stroke, and I tell her so.

We go to visit the cemetery while we're in Connecticut. My mother gets out of the car and walks haltingly, finding her father's grave by some internal honing device.

The sun is hot white, bleaching everything it can find. Kneeling carefully in the grass, she lifts her right hand to shade her eyes, and grips the gravestone with her left. Her papery skin shrouds the fine bones of her hands. She squints, smiling up at the camera and I cringe at the grass stains that must be forming at her knees. There is an innocence in her expression, as if to say: *I'm here! Hello! I'm not dead!*

---

4   Marshall, *Elizabeth Bishop*

There was a period in high school when I fantasized about my mother dying, killing her even. It was almost daily, this wanting her dead, our heated competition. Now, I can't get enough of her.

My mother will never truly understand my alcoholism. She has survived by her indomitable will.

I have a will for drink.

V

Recently, my father and I have been digitizing old family slides. First, we preview them. I sit on the blue couch, my face inches from the glowing white wall. My mother gazes out at us in Technicolor, glorious, her smile a knowing confidence I have never felt. She is wearing beautiful plaid pants nipped in at the waist. I want to crawl into the wall and wear her skin, to feel the colors she bathes in. I want to drink her in.

I try to conjure the pain that Bishop felt, not having her mother to fuss over her, to antagonize her, this greedy intimacy I take for granted. When I return home from my parent's house, everything, even my skin, smells like my mother. Not some organic, unkempt smell, but a perfume that clings, that is only perceptible when you are away from it.

I imagine Elizabeth Bishop longing for this scent of mothering, and drinking and drinking and drinking to find it.

The Earring
Anya Ravitz

In the summer of 2008, a month after receiving my undergraduate diploma and flipping the tassel of my mortarboard to the left, my boyfriend came to me with a proposal of marriage. Against every feminist lesson about autonomy I had been taught both at home and at school, I accepted. I was deliriously happy and believed nothing could destroy this bliss. My euphoria lasted approximately three weeks.

We returned from our honeymoon and began to argue. Or, rather, he began to argue with me. Little things bugged him: I was too tired after work, I didn't want to go to parties on weeknights, I woke him when I left our bed to run in the mornings. And so, I compromised. I ran after work and then stayed up late watching movies or spending time with his friends. I was tired during the day and my job performance suffered, but tension at home dissipated. These tiffs were surrounded by good times, like apple picking or taking long walks around the local lake, and I was happy to reframe our discord as the normal growing pains of marriage. Except growth never manifested.

Instead, my world darkened, although I pretended otherwise to friends and family. I was ashamed of my rash decision to marry and could only imagine their derision when they discovered I had failed. In fear and self-protection, I isolated myself. I stopped returning phone calls and texts and emails from friends. I stopped visiting my mom. I came home directly after work and made excuses to avoid socializing. I kept conversations light, superficial. I painted a picture of how I thought I should feel, the way my marriage worked in my fantasies: happy adventures and meaningful conversations; satisfaction and peace.

Just as fights about whose responsibility it is to turn out the light or take out the trash or empty the dishwasher are never about their menial subjects, so our squabbles about my work schedule and energy levels were a front for deeper unrest.

Contributing to our unhappiness were several decisions I made years earlier. I ended our relationship after seven months because he was depressed and I was not prepared to handle that large emotion. We stopped talking then and began our separate lives. We had mutual friends so remained aware of each other's existence but neither attempted to reconnect. He began dating and I decided instead to have a series of one-night stands. I also decided, while visiting a friend on summer vacation, to have the cartilage in my right ear pierced with a blue stud.

Although these two acts—my piercing and my sexual encounters—were separate in time, location, and mindset, they became linked in his vision of my identity. The earring that to me symbolized memories with my best friend, to him symbolized the other men with whom I had slept. Though he said he forgave me for having sex while we were separated, he found the earring intolerable.

With the earring in, I was a *slut, whore, bitch.* I was the reason trust eroded in our relationship. The earring meant I was looking for more partners. The earring was my siren song.

Anything can gain the aura of truth when repeated enough times and with enough bravado. I tucked my conviction of my selfhood in a safe space, deep inside my mind, too removed to disrupt my current environment but retrievable in the future. I filled the space from this autonomy with new beliefs—his beliefs. I now believed him when he said I had betrayed his love. I now believed him when he asserted I should have saved myself for him, even during the year we were not together. I now believed him when he said I could absolve myself, but only if I removed the earring.

Part of my willful dissonance was perpetuated by fear. I worried I would be abandoned by the few people left in my personal life. I did not understand that people who love me will support my decisions, especially when they take me out of unhealthy relationships. I did not understand forgiveness, of self and of others. All I knew was how poorly I had treated good friends and family, how little I had shared with them, and how untruthful I had been about the realities of my daily life. I was ashamed.

I imagined their rage—not at him but at me—when they discovered I had allowed myself to be abused. When they realized I did not assert my right to be treated fairly. Or that I had chosen to subsume myself in a man.

All I could feel was my own pain. There was no room for compassion. I was unable to look outside myself or to envision a different future. I had made my choice and I was prepared to endure.

I converted to this new ideology that condemned any trace of my life without him. As proof of loyalty, I wiggled off the backing and pulled the stud out of its hole in my cartilage. I did not throw away the earring, rather I hid it in the bottom of my jewelry box.

Sometimes, if he was not at home, I opened the box, rummaged around beneath tangled necklaces, and located the disgraced piece. Taking it in my fingers quickly, before sentimentality and tears could set in, I slipped the rod into place, feel it secure and safe. My hidden act of rebellion.

I stopped this practice after a while, when regaining my autonomy felt futile and absurd. What did my ritual accomplish, anyhow? Even without the earring, I was *slut, whore, bitch*. Even without the earring, I did not deserve his forgiveness. I had dared explore my sexuality without him and, he decreed, through actions and accusations, taking power away from him was unforgivable. Left fallow for a few months, the hole in my ear healed closed. Acceptance was the only way to survive.

I cannot remember the exact moment my hope for change coalesced from a nascent thought into a driving force in my decision-making. Possibly it was the night his plans for sleeping in our bed with his girlfriend while I slept on the couch were complicated when they came home to find me having a glass of wine with a friend from work. Although he was comfortable sharing infidelity within the confines of our relationship, he was less willing to expose his behavior to outsiders. He poured my friend drink after drink, thinking (he told me later) she would feel drunk and leave. When she finally protested she was too drunk to drive home and asked to spend the night, he left us both on the couch while he bedded down with his lover. The next morning, filled with shame, I explained my situation.

I told her how my marriage had devolved into a power-struggle that he always won. I explained the abuse, his affair, my hopelessness. I braced myself for a lecture on asserting my rights, feminist power, and leaving the relationship without hesitation. Instead, she provided understanding.

Over the next few months, she encouraged me to spend time away from him and our apartment. I told my story to other co-workers. They also understood. To my amazement, there was no rage, no sternness, no disappointment. Instead, I found support and comfort.

My friend encouraged me to move into a new apartment with her. We found a place a few towns over and I told my husband I was moving out. I expected encouragement. He had spent countless hours convincing me to leave him, asserting I would be better off on my own. He had proposed annulment, coerced me into trying to have an affair with a coworker (thankfully that was a failure), and told me stories of the great professional successes his former partners all achieved when they left their relationship with him. I had stayed on through all these attempts, against his purported wishes. To the news I was leaving, however, he only had fury and a list of reasons I would fail.

My resolve to leave and stay gone was tested a few months later. I was sick with a head cold in my new apartment. I had an unexpected night off from my waitressing job. My roommate was out of town. I had just cuddled down on the couch with a warm blanket, tea, and mindless television, preparing to go to bed early and sleep for as long as possible when his girlfriend called.

He was drunk, she explained, and would not move indoors out of the freezing winter rain without me. I refused. I wanted to have my night alone, relaxing into the peace of my own company.

She begged me to help. I could hear him crying on the other side of the phone. They both sounded miserable. I should have been happy. I should have thought, "Now they get what they deserve. Now they can suffer together." Instead, some bit of loyalty or common decency broke free and I said, "Fine. I'll be there in twenty minutes."

When I arrived, he was stumbling and shouting my name into the rain. The apartment was above a block of storefronts and accessed only by walking through a flower shop. The girlfriend walked back to her car as I struggled to heave him along the narrow walkway between plants without breaking any pots.

He became more lucid on his couch with a glass of water, though still quite inebriated. He had gone to a bar and drunk endless vodka-and-sodas until the bartender cut him off and he had to call his girlfriend. The whole time, he repeated, he had talked to the bartender about missing me—as though that made it true.

He apologized for his behavior throughout our marriage. He promised to change. He even said he would call my parents to explain that he was at fault. "You can make the rules," he asserted. "I will do anything you tell me."

I wanted to believe. To release the stress of the past eighteen months in one long exhale. I imagined placing my head on his chest and sinking into the couch, resuming the comfort of marriage. Simplicity.

In this fantasy, life assumed a steady calm. I would not have to go to sleep alone each night or negotiate a cleaning schedule with my roommate. He and I would talk with honesty, go to therapy, grow. We would have a real relationship.

And then my mind focused back on the room, on his assertions of apology and contrition. I remembered I was sick and instead of going to bed early, relaxing into the pleasures of single life, I was sitting on a sagging brown couch in a dirty cramped apartment in front of a large-screen television purchased for him with the last of my good credit. This was not my apartment. His body was not for my comfort.

A few nights later, I sat in a bar recounting this incident to a friend. She assumed I had accepted his apology and was preparing to make things work. I turned to my friend and said, "No. I am done with that fucker."

My hope for change grew steadily over the years as I created a routine without him. I made new friends, started new jobs, and moved to new apartments. I felt my confidence grow. A small part of myself remained hidden, however, buried beneath the layers of my mind, where I had placed it for safekeeping during my marriage.

Several years later, after I moved from Boston, to Los Angeles, to Wisconsin, to Chicago, searching for work and for identity, and after I started to feel a tiny shred of myself reemerge in the form of writing and goal-setting, my best friend decided to pierce her nose.

She had recently broken up with her long-term boyfriend and wanted to celebrate. When she asked me to accompany her, I remembered my own, now six-years-healed, cartilage piercing.

I wanted to complete my healing by embodying the woman I was before my marriage crushed my feminist identity. A woman who was strong, made her own decisions, and took care of her body in any way that felt appropriate. Piercing a new hole into the smooth skin of my right ear was a step toward reclaiming this woman.

I had put aside my values when they clashed with my husband's because I had entered an agreement of love and support, and I thought that meant standing by my decision forever. I was too ashamed and too attached to the memories of love to admit I had made a mistake. I did not know how to change my situation nor would I have been willing to make changes, had they been presented.

My pilgrimage to the tattoo parlor was transformative. As I walked through the doors of the shop, I was flooded with excitement and relief. Soon I would have physical proof that I was moving forward. I smiled as I chose a small blue stud from the array of potential earrings on display. I felt my heart race with anticipation as I walked toward the piercing room. I was ready.

When I told the man doing the piercing about the significance of this new earring, he laughed. "Good riddance," he said, and, "You are better off without him." His laughter was therapeutic and invited the hidden part of myself to emerge. And so, it unfolded with curiosity from the corner of my mind. I was ready to move on with my life.

Every time I glimpse my piercing in the mirror or absentmindedly touch the stud while thinking, reading, writing, living my life, I remember: I control my identity.

Lazy Bottom Retreats:
Where No One is Actually Lazy or a Bottom

By Lazy Bottom Retreat Members:
Anne Swenson Ticknor, Paige Averett, Allison Crowe,
Anna Froula, Cynthia A. Grace-McCaskey, Amanda Ann Klein,
Jennifer F. McKinnon, Stacy L. Weiss, and Amber Wigent

This essay amplifies the story of nine women to weave together personal reflections of finding each other and reconnecting with ourselves through a
bi-annual pilgrimage to a nearby beach. Through each pilgrimage we are
fulfilled and strengthened—individually and collectively—professionally,
personally, and socially. Our combined story of pilgrimage began in spring
of 2015 when upon meeting we quickly organized ourselves as a means of
personal and professional survival. Each of us was looking for and needed
women like ourselves who understood challenges in balancing work with
home, academia, and the tenure process.

    Our pilgrimage began with a front porch gathering. While we knew
each other in smaller groupings, we did not create our beach pilgrimage until after we all united and found our name: Lazy Bottoms. Our porch happy hour, turned into several happy hours of drinking wine, sharing stories about our personal and professional lives, and realizing as Anna put
it, that we had finally "found our people." As comfort settled in, or maybe it was the wine, our conversation turned to sex and relationships. Paige
shared about a relationship she had just begun with a woman, and some of
the sexually fluid women in our group began discussing roles and relationships with both men and women. The idea of being a lazy bottom was discussed. According to Urban Dictionary a lazy bottom is a term *"commonly*

used amongst lesbians referring to a pillow princess that is boring on the bottom."[1] This idea quickly moved away from sexual behaviors to recognizing the irony in any one of us actually being a lazy bottom, as none of us are lazy in any aspect of our daily lives. Instead we are highly productive activists, rebels, motivators, employees, partners, and organizers. At the same time, the idea of being a (non-sexual) lazy bottom immensely spoke to our need for self-care, time to rest, and need for others to sometimes take the lead. Thus, the Lazy Bottoms were formed.

We shared a deep desire to find a space to have time to sit and process what we knew or were learning away from distractions in our daily lives. Jen pitched the idea of going out of town for a writing retreat. At first there was slight hesitation. The whole experience felt indulgent beyond belief. How would we be able to carve out the time to go away from our work and our families for an entire weekend? Who were we to go out of town in order to sit and think for eight uninterrupted hours? And, how were we supposed to write when at the beach with newfound girlfriends and a lot of wine? This idea was especially challenging for the two new mothers in the group, Jen and Allison. When Jen said, "When you're ready, I'll be ready," it created space for Allison to consider that she could be ready. Allison remembers pedaling home to breastfeed her new baby, even though what she really wanted to do was stay on the front porch and dream up a weekend writing retreat. All of us wanted our newly found friendships to continue and knew that if we could spend a weekend together, we'd become the supportive community we'd been looking for and desperately hoping to find. Similarly, Amanda found that, after many years of motherhood, carving out large chunks of uninterrupted work time continued to be nearly impossible at home. She had ideas for her second book but wasn't able to move past short bursts of writing that did not cohere with each other until the writing retreats offered her time without incessant knocks on the door so that she could finally finish a book project that was conceived and completed on the retreats.

Within a few months the first Lazy Bottom Retreat was realized with seven of the women from the porch. Jen and Allison were ready. Jen called us to the table to find a date and agreed to investigate writing a grant that

---

1   Justy65. "Lazy Bottom," *Urban Dictionary*, May 19, 2016, https://www.urbandictionary.com/define.php?term=lazy%20bottom.

would hopefully fund our first writing retreat housing (it did not). Jen persisted and booked us a house on the beach. As the retreats and years progressed, we believed there were others like us whom we had not yet found, and we were right. Three more women joined our bi-annual pilgrimage, including a woman working as a nurse in a regional hospital, which is also the primary teaching hospital for our local university, who helps remind us that first and foremost, we must take care of ourselves as individuals.

In terms of logistics and routine of our pilgrimage, the writing retreats began as a Friday afternoon to Sunday morning, and quickly evolved to a Thursday afternoon to Sunday morning. We are highly organized and cooperative, which means we take turns finding a large house at the beach in the off-season to rent, carpooling, planning meals, dividing the labor, designing our writing and/or life projects, and bringing items for work and play. Each day starts with goal setting before quiet uninterrupted work time, breaking for meals signaled by ringing the Lazy Bottom brass bell. The first two evenings include a celebration of accomplishments and a creative group project. The projects bring on laughter, storytelling, life sharing, and deepening intimacy. On the final night of our collective journey, we celebrate our productivity and renewed sense of self with dinner at a restaurant before taking over a karaoke bar that has led to us being infamous with the owners and among some of the locals.

Finding Our Shared Identity

Our story illustrates a deepened understanding of feminism through a shared community of women who are highly intelligent, supportive, motivated, organized, and determined. Although we are in different disciplines, we have much in common. The academics have PhDs and significant others who followed us for our jobs. We live in a small city with often conservative political, religious, and regional beliefs. We all share liberal political and social justice beliefs with feminist theory guiding us. We do not fit *in* to the place, but we fit *with* one another. Across the group, many overlap in their experiences of growing up to reject organized religion as adolescents, rebel against family ideals of traditional feminine norms, resist oppression, and/or recognize sexual fluidity. Our overlapping and intersectional identities both strengthen bonds within a supportive community as well as diversify our advocacy as women living in a conservative, southern, mid-sized city.

Our bi-annual pilgrimage to the beach provides each of us dedicated time and space to support one another as women within a confluence of responsibilities and demands at work and home. Although each of us are in different stages of life (ranging from recently married or divorced to long-term partnerships; newly mothered, older children, and childfree; long-term academics, first appointments, and third careers), each of us have found and provided collective strength through discussing shared interests and goals; have collaborated on research, writing, and life projects; and celebrated each other's successes as academics and as women. Three main veins run through our pilgrimage: navigating academic life as women, engaging in self-care to renew and revive, and deepening our sense of feminism within a community of kick-ass women.

Navigating Academic Life as Women

We represent a diversity of disciplines, interests, and career stages, and our experiences as practitioners, care-takers, teachers, and researchers offer each of us a unique perspective as women in various stages of becoming professors. Both informal and formal mentoring and collaboration opportunities are present at each retreat to the beach. More experienced academics (those with tenure, those who have more than one university placement, those who undertake particular research, etc.) offer guidance about the tenure process, research methodologies, grant writing, publication process, navigating the politics of academia, and teaching methods. Although most of us focus on uninterrupted work time for our academic positions, Amber uses the writing retreats to nurture certain skills that fill her soul with happiness, like cooking and being artistic, or to complete projects as a parent volunteer at her child's school.

Several of us work in male dominated fields, are isolated in our individual research pursuits, and/or have never been a part of an academic community. The retreats benefit each of us with the collective experiences and knowledge we have garnered over our careers—not just as academics, but as women struggling to balance work, partners, family, and personal needs in a world that continues to be dominated by the rules and desires of older white men. The time and space to talk and think deeply with other women about the unique demands and challenges of being a woman in academia helps to demystify the politics and processes while adding a sense of belonging to a larger community of women.

Stacy, who joined the group as a tenure-track faculty member still getting her footing as a researcher, found it was initially incredibly hard to listen to others go around the table on the first night of the retreat, hearing about amazing projects and updates on how they were progressing with what seemed like great ease. However, as she talked about her plans and ideas, she discovered that she did, in fact, know what needed to be done and how to start. As she participated in the first few retreats, she started to hear and observe others, as they worked through their messy and complicated projects, and how the talking became part of the process.

Two grant-funded projects exemplify the collaboration across disciplines made possible by the writing retreats. Anna and Jen found that they were both considering applying to the same initiative to 1) support a transition program for the student veterans (Anna) and 2) support military families and veterans on a Pacific island (Jen). Anne, somewhat facetiously, inquired how the project might include her, and quickly a cross-disciplinary project spanning maritime studies, education, and war and film studies was in the works. The planning and drafting continued beyond the retreat and because both applications received funding, a spin-off feminist pilgrimage to the Pacific occurred the following summer, which then deeply enriched the transition program at home.

Depending on the discipline, we may not be encouraged to collaborate on projects at our university, so there isn't always someone to celebrate when we hit a career milestone. But because we understand the academy and have the chance to talk about our projects during the retreat, we can support and celebrate each other in ways that others who are close to us may not be able to. There is a slippery slope involved in not celebrating—moving on quickly to the "next thing" or even beginning to believe that accomplishments (large and small) are not worthy of recognition or reward—so making time to celebrate each other and our accomplishments is particularly important.

Engaging in Self-care to Renew and Revive

We need self-care, reflection, and time away to consider what refuels our passions and energies. We are at different stages in our personal lives and that means that our family responsibilities are evolving and changing in ways that can complicate, challenge, and deplete us emotionally. We are reminded, and strongly encouraged by Amber, to engage in silent retreat time aimed at clearing headspace from our daily lives and responsibilities to really connect with ourselves. Our pilgrimage to a beach *away* from our homes enables us to do this.

The retreat also provides a unique opportunity for engaging in creative and relaxing pursuits that we do not typically have the opportunity to explore during our day to day routines. These activities are similar to when women would make baskets and quilts, grind grains or make bread together and provide close intimate times to share and reflect in the safety and friendship of the other women. The projects often involve one member of the group sharing or bringing an activity to the group, which builds a sense of community to have others engage and support each other as we participate in these shared social experiences. The shared activities are often linked to personal or intimate experiences from our child or adulthood who have made us the women we are today. Art projects have involved nostalgic materials, such as Shrinky Dinks, to create empowering and affirming art and jewelry. We have laughed and gossiped over make-up, face masks, and press-on nails, creating personas and trying on personalities like we did, or in some cases did not do, as adolescents. Group members have brought their interests and talents to help others gain insights into themselves or finding calm through discussing dreams, exploring aromatherapy, reading tarot cards, or discussing animal spirit books to ponder our primal identities. We have shared insight into our past selves through reading aloud old love letters, girlhood notes, and diaries; sharing home videos; and talking about our decisions and choices in life over a bottle of wine while sitting on the porch or taking a long walk on the beach. Physical exercise is also another part of our self-care focus. At our pilgrimage, we make time for yoga, walking on the beach, running, and exercise videos. This uninterrupted time is vastly different than the more typical attempts at fitting in a discussion at a local social gathering or making time for exercise. The beach is a safe and uninterrupted space without partners or children.

Our journey to the beach is not complete until we celebrate, let loose, and mark the end of our pilgrimage with karaoke fun. We dress according to a previously agreed-upon theme (80s night was a big hit) and take on personas, ensuring that we fully escape our daily lives, to joyously sing karaoke and dance. It is cathartic in so many ways—leaving behind a productive weekend, celebrating our accomplishments, and preparing to come home to our normal routines. Self-care is important because it helps us remember that what is most important to *us* is the happiness of ourselves and our families, and that is much more important than reaching goals deter-mined by others for our jobs.

Deepening our Sense of Feminism within a Community of Kick-Ass Women

Each of us considers ourselves feminists, champions of and advocates for women to be successful, productive, and supported. Several of us are rais-ing children and want all of our children to see each of us as the strong, de-termined, organized, intelligent, successful, and supported women we are. In both our professional and personal lives, we are advocates for ourselves, each other, and other women in academia and the workforce. We know the challenges, road blocks, insecurity, and isolation that can saturate women, and, together, we have found that each pilgrimage to the beach provides us collective and individual strength and courage to uplift and affirm each other, ourselves, and other women. Each retreat provides us the opportuni-ty to celebrate, commiserate, and revive each other in ways that only wom-en can do for each other.

We have shared information about our pilgrimage and journey with our colleagues, and some have started their own writing retreats based on our model. We love that our idea, and Jen's determination to book our first retreat weekend, is spreading. Our group has now expanded to ten women. However, we do not invite all interested parties into our inner circle. Cin-dy shared that she valued our community even more when she realized that while we encourage others to form their own groups, we do not look for others to come to the retreat just to fill up beds and reduce the costs. Instead we each have chosen one another, and each contribute something meaning-ful to the benefit of the other women in our community.

Our supportive community extends beyond our journeys to the beach by spending time together outside the workday (happy hours, pot-lucks, nights on the town, etc.). We keep in communication through group text and video messaging. Since most of us work together at the Universi-ty and live in the same neighborhood, we have created a network of knowl-edge, access, and awareness. We regularly consult with each other about university matters to provide information, ask questions, and share per-spectives. We network within the committees that govern our university. We also check-in for support on projects or hard conversations with col-leagues or students. We use our group messaging for political organizing in election season, to personally connect, organize childcare, plan gatherings, and share the details of our lives. Each member of our group is an expert and has unique knowledge and information to share and answer our queries. Collectively we represent education, social work, counseling, nursing, anthropology, history/maritime studies, English/film studies, and now biology. Together we are trying to make our university and city more equitable and our feminist pilgrimage to the beach provides us the space, strength, and power to enact our collective vision.

Finally, a note about our writing process for this project. The act of writing, reading, rereading, revising, and editing this essay provided us a chance to reflect on the depth of self-care each pilgrimage to the beach allowed. Each of us wrote our reflections and read each other's reflections separately. We shared our writing via email and processed the content through group messaging. Most of us reported crying as we thought, wrote, and read our words and each other's words as we once again reminded ourselves how important and special our writing retreats are. As Audre Lorde reminds us, "Caring for myself is not self-indulgence, it is self-preservation, and that is an act of political warfare."[2] We are a collective group of political women warriors who actively seek self-preservation for ourselves and our sisters.

---

2   Audre Lorde, *A Burst of Light: And Other Essays* [Kindle Edition] (Ithaca, NY: Firebrand Books, 1988), 130, Location 1702.

Books and Travels: A Feminist Journey

Holiday Vega

I consider many of my travels to have been feminist pilgrimages, but what made them feminist in nature were the women I met, developed friendships with, and read books with. I traveled to India in 2012 and met an incredible, inspiring woman named Ama Adhe who survived torture over decades when she was imprisoned by the Chinese in occupied Tibet, her home country. Upon gaining freedom, she used her voice to tell the truth and to help and empower others. When I met with her, with a group of other students, she told us she still has nightmares. I myself have survived trauma and still have posttraumatic stress disorder from the sexual abuse I endured. To hear that this woman still has nightmares after all these decades, and has the strength to continue to tell her story to help and empower the Tibetan people shocked and inspired me.

While in India, I also befriended a Tibetan refugee named Pilar.* I gave her a book to help her improve her English: *Pippi Longstocking* by Astrid Lindgren.[1] At the time I had just begun reading *The Girl with the Dragon Tattoo* by Stieg Larsson[2] and the parallels between these two fictional characters, Pippi Longstocking and Lisbeth Salander, both girls with no parents who harness rare talents—in Pippi's case, incredible strength, and in Lisbeth's case, genius-level computer hacking skills, and between myself and Pilar were striking. Pilar left Chinese occupied Tibet when she

---

1   Astrid Lindgren, *Pippi Longstocking* (Oxford: Oxford University Press, 1945/2002).

2   Stieg Larsson, *The Girl with the Dragon Tattoo* (New York: NY, Vintage Books, 2009).

was twelve years old to escape to India. She has not been able to contact her family since then. I also had not been in contact with my family for many years, though for vastly different reasons: my parents were abusive. Although Pilar and I both navigate the world without family, completely alone, I will never understand what it is like to be a refugee in another country. I bear the scars of prolonged trauma.

In another part of the world, at the Grand Canyon, when I was traveling alone across the United States, I met another solo female traveler, Arrow.* We exchanged stories of the sexist expectations strangers would express to us during our travels. People would be horrified or shocked to learn that I, a young woman, was traveling completely by myself. Arrow had this same experience as a solo female traveler and we expressed frustration at the fact that men traveling alone never get asked about it. People never lecture men about the "dangers of traveling alone." People never ask them, "What do your parents think?" For me, this in particular was a retraumatizing question as it was a reminder of my abusive parents and how little they care for my life. In a feminist world, there would be no gendered expectation for who is able to travel alone.

Arrow and I have stayed in touch and exchanged books, she gifting me *Into the Wild*,[3] the journal of a young man who traveled alone and died (a little bit of irony there) and I gifted her *The Girl with All the Gifts* by Mike Carey.[4] At the Grand Canyon she told me about her fascination with zombies and about a paper she'd written on the topic. This book was not written with feminist intention, but both Arrow and I talked about nerd culture (like video games and zombies) and how this is a subculture usually considered to be one created by and for men. *The Girl with All the Gifts* features a black teacher and a young zombie girl, both marginalized and oppressed, who learn from and empower each other.

Another friend of mine, Sophie*, traveled with me across seven countries in Asia. There were places, such as Malaysia and Singapore, where Sophie would put on a makeshift headscarf, though she is not Muslim, in order to be permitted to enter certain mosques. I declined to join her. Sophie and I had many conversations on our almost month-long adventure

---

3   John Krakauer, *Into the Wild* (New York: NY: Anchor Books, 1996).

4   Mike Carey, *The Girl with All the Gifts* (New York, NY: Orbit Hachette Book Group, 2014).

together about what it means to be feminist. We both identify as feminist, and we both believe that sexism and sexist oppression is wrong. However, Sophie feels that women should be treated equally, and therefore they should be given the same expectations as men and not be given anything extra just on the basis of being female, and she expressed this thought as applied to minority ethnic groups as well. I don't agree with that, and Sophie did express that she does feel that structural change is necessary to make things equal. Until sexism and racism no longer exist, I believe we have an obligation to give "extra" to those oppressed groups, to make up for the inequality that exists.

Though Sophie and I both enjoy reading and writing, we tend to talk more about movies and television shows than about books. We watch *Game of Thrones* and express whether it's feminist or not, and we both enjoy anime, including Miyazaki's Studio Ghibli films. During our trip across Asia we initially intended to visit the Studio Ghibli Museum in Tokyo and we watched Studio Ghibli films in preparation, although we ultimately did not end up going.

Sophie and I discussed why Hayao Miyazaki would write so many strong girl protagonists, and I expressed suspicion about his focus on young girls. I tend to be suspicious of men's intentions and tend to err on the side of believing men's actions are nefarious in nature. This is not feminist, and it has nothing to do with feminism. It's because of my past. I was sexually abused and assaulted by many different men, and this has caused me to be distrustful and skeptical, especially with older men and little girls. But this way of thinking and being a feminist is challenging: if I am honest about my suspicions and fears of men, I paint myself as the classic man-hating feminist. How cruel: men get to abuse us, rape us, and then call us man-hating if we call out this abuse as part of a system of patriarchal oppression.

Sophie thought perhaps Miyazaki might have daughters and wanted to tell stories to inspire them, but we looked it up later and found out he only has sons and grandsons. *A Song of Ice and Fire*,[5] the series of books that inspired *Game of Thrones*, were also written by a man (George R. R. Martin), and *Buffy the Vampire Slayer* (Joss Whedon), another show with a strong female lead, was also written by a man. It's wonderful that stories are

---

5   George R. R. Martin, *A Song of Ice and Fire* (London: HarperVoyager, 2011).

being told by men about strong, brave, inspiring women, but I was ready to make a change and find similarly powerful works by women writers.

When I moved to Hawaiʻi I joined a Books by Women book club that made me reflect on the media I consume. The book club, created by a well-read feminist woman who has become a great friend of mine, began because one year she wanted to read only books by women. She created the book club to lead others to read books by women and consider why, although most writers are women, most of the awards and bestsellers are written by men. Although J. K. Rowling still holds the position of the wealthiest author of all time, and created a legacy with her Harry Potter series, her books feature a male main protagonist. For this book club, we mostly read fiction although we did read a memoir *Redefining Realness*,[6] written by a transgender black woman, Janet Mock, who grew up in Hawaiʻi, and a book called *Freshwater*[7] by a Nigerian woman Akwaeke Emezi, and though the book is categorized as fiction, it is heavily based upon the author's own experiences.

For the first time, I found myself noticing things that had escaped my attention before. I noticed how many video games I play are created by men (all of them), and how many movies I've seen and shows I love that were written by and directed by men (a LOT of them). I would question myself before reading a book by a man, and started to seek out books written by women. I started listening to female-only music playlists, one created by my feminist friend who created the Books by Women book club. I noticed that on my tea, chamomile and valerian root, there were quotes on the teabags and all of them had been written by men. I use an app called Momentum on my web browser and every day it has a background of a different part of the world and a different quote. I noticed that more often than not, these quotes were words written or spoken by men. Across my world travels, I grew the most in Hawaiʻi, learning from my feminist friends. Though I always identified as feminist I didn't start really reading any books about feminist theory until Hawaiʻi. I started reading the works of bell hooks and Audre Lorde and Roxane Gay. I learned about intersectional feminism and the ways that racism and sexism are related and separate. I started noticing the lack of women of color represented in media as well. I recognized my

---

6   Janet Mock, *Redefining Realness: My Path to Womanhood, Identity, Love, & So Much More* (New York, NY: Simon & Schuster, 2015).

7   Akwaeke Emezi, *Freshwater* (New York, NY: Grove Press, 2018).

own privilege as a white educated woman from the United States. I have far more opportunities than so many people. I recognize the injustice in this.

One conversation I remember having with my friends and one of my professors here is: who is allowed to tell these stories? Can white authors write about the Native Hawaiian experience, or the black experience? Can men who have never been abused write stories about girls who have been sexually abused? These are important questions to deeply reflect on. We were considering books like *Haoles in Hawai'i*,[8] written by a white/haole author, Judy Rohrer from the mainland about what the word haole means in Hawai'i, and *My Absolute Darling*,[9] a fiction book written by a man, Gabriel Tallent, who as far as we know was never abused or assaulted in any way, about a girl who is sexually abused by her father. I have learned how to critique books and other forms of media from an intersectional feminist perspective.

While many of my friends here in Hawai'i are librarians, and we advocate against censorship as a general rule, we also believe in access to accurate information. We often debate what materials we should order, and if we are obligated to order materials that advocate for hatred, violence, sexism, or racism. We discussed a book titled *Feminist Pedagogy for Library Instruction* by Maria T. Accardi[10] in a library reading group we host here, and for the first time I had a map to all the ways I could incorporate feminism, and intersectional feminism, into my professional practice. I looked into the author's blog and read that she is also a survivor of sexual abuse. At the time, I marveled at her comfort with self-disclosing that. Again, I felt inspired by the courage of another woman to speak the truth and call out something terrible.

Feminism is often perceived in a negative light or seen as some man-hating club. Everywhere I've ever traveled to, though my experience is limited, I've encountered opposition because of that word. I am a feminist. Although I tend to fear men, because of my traumatic past, I do not hate them. On my travels, my pilgrimages to many places, and through my

---

8   Judy Rohrer, *Haoles in Hawai'i* (Honolulu, HI: University of Hawaii Press, 2000).

9   Gabriel Tallent, *My Absolute Darling* (New York, NY: Riverhead Books, 2017).

10   Maria T. Accardi, *Feminist Pedagogy for Library Instruction* (Sacramento, Library Juice Press, 2013).

conversations with people, I have started learning how to untangle my feminist identity, values, and beliefs, from what thoughts and fears I have based on my experience of having been abused by men.

I believe feminism is about ending sexist oppression and all the ways that it is enacted. I believe that rape, female genital mutilation, and other acts of violence against women and girls are aspects of how sexism is practiced across the world. To deny that women and girls face more violence, particularly sexual violence, than men, is to deny reality. We don't yet live in an equal world. And while, certainly, there are men who have been sexually abused or raped, or who have experienced violence, that isn't evidence that sexism no longer exists, as these acts of violence are still overwhelmingly enacted against women and girls. Beyond that, when women or girls do come forward, they are often not believed, unless you gather together hundreds of mostly white women and girls to speak out, as in some recent criminal cases involving a Hollywood director and a USA Gymnastics doctor. One girl's voice alone is silenced, and even in the history of these criminal cases which eventually ended in a conviction, when only one girl came forward, she was silenced.

The main thing I have learned across the many places I have traveled to: if you don't have a voice, you can't change anything. There are still many places in the world where women and girls are silenced in a myriad of ways.

And here I return to the start of my journey; before I could go on a physical pilgrimage, I went on pilgrimages through reading. Writing is one way of using our voice. One of the first books I remember reading as a child that I have traced back to some of my feminist thinking was *The House on Mango Street* by Sandra Cisneros.[11] This book gave voice to what I could not yet speak. Girls are taught, just by growing up, that our bodies do not belong to us and we are not safe in this world.

I would not learn the words for the concepts this book taught me until many years later: intersectional feminism, structural oppression, systemic racism, sexism. I would read books recommended to me by feminist friends, talking about feminism while hiking up Pu'u Pia on O'ahu, or in Dharamsala at the kora trail around the Dalai Lama temple. This included

---

11   Sandra Cisneros, *The House on Mango Street* (New York: NY: Vintage Contemporaries, 2009).

Feminism Is for Everybody by bell hooks[12] and *Living a Feminist Life* by Sara Ahmed,[13] recommended amidst talks about settler colonialism in Hawai'i and refugee rights in India.

But feminism isn't just about ending the most horrific ways that sexist oppression is enacted. Feminism is about calling out all of the "little" nonviolent actions that create a society where such violence is practiced. It's about calling out each instance of sexism when it is enacted through words or actions. Being a feminist takes a great deal of courage. Speaking up about these "little" instances of sexism is almost always met with opposition. And yet it is necessary that we speak and use our voice. I've learned over my feminist journey that it is only by using our voice that we can create change, empower others, and truly enact feminist values.

* indicates pseudonym

---

12 bell hooks, *Feminism Is for Everybody: Passionate Politics* (Cambridge, MA: South End, 2000).

13 Sara Ahmed, *Living a Feminist Life* (Durham, NC: Duke University Press, 2017).

Cycling as Adventure and Encounter
Alison Stankrauff

Bicycling is so many things to me. It's my way to explore, my way to feel strong on both the inside and the outside, my way to connect with my community and communities far beyond, my way to exercise, and much more. Cycling is something that helps me to keep evolving, both within myself and in the knowledge of the world beyond me. I love the strength and self-intuition that cycling gives me.

I am by profession an academic. I'm an archivist and librarian, which means that I see the world through a historic and informational lens. This absolutely applies to my work life, but it also applies to my personal or "civilian" life. Having worked on university campuses throughout my professional career (three to date), I am surrounded in my "nine to five" life with people from all over the world who are doing fascinating and important research, writing, teaching, and learning in disciplines that cover the full range of knowledge. That is my weekly and yearly framework that keeps me pointed toward wanting to know more about the world and just how we—and I—fit into it. Or how it looks without me in it too!

I am a deeply curious person. I always want to know more about the world around me—whether that is my own neighborhood, my city, my state—or in places much further beyond. I am fascinated by the how and why things are the way that they are. That fascination with the present means also a much-related fascination with the past. The two go hand in hand for me.

I've been able to find an amazing conveyance for this curiosity in cycling. Cycling allows me to get out into the world and to learn on a daily basis—even if it's small things. Sometimes it's large things.

I bike every day to and from work. In the warm months (I do live in the Heartland, after all), I extend those rides after work and on the weekends to as many miles as time and daylight allow.

I am a proud Midwesterner. I live in Detroit, a city that I feel deeply connected to. I have lived in other cities and towns that I feel a similar connection—South Bend, Indiana; Yellow Springs, Ohio; and many others. One thing that makes me feel connected to these places that I've called home is the close exploration that comes of a place and a community through cycling.

Cycling also makes me feel stronger as a woman. It allows me to inhabit a space—a set of spaces and places—as a woman. This has given me opportunities to learn not only about places, but it has contributed to me learning about myself.

I am a life-long traveler. Traveling feeds my curiosity about the world and allows me to keep learning and growing and expanding. My preferred method of traveling is via bicycle. I have been traveling in other countries via bicycle since age twelve. I have cycled in Vietnam, Sri Lanka, Mexico, Iceland, Bulgaria, France, the Netherlands, Britain, Canada, and extensively in the United States (fig. 1 Bulgaria in 2016 at the port at Varna; fig. 2 Bulgaria in 2016 at the Black Sea; and fig. 3 Icelandic cycling in 2017).

I've had some terrific cycling trips with friends. Cycling solo or with friends is all about exploration and adventure. Ultimately, though, I have

Figure 1

to say that I prefer to travel via bicycle solo. This is when my cycling adventures are the most free.

One of the foremost qualities of cycling is this freedom that it affords me. It's exhilarating and empowering to make my own decisions about where to go, when to go, where to stop (or not), how fast or slow to go, etc., etc. That's freedom! (I write this in the depths of winter, which has its own beauty, but it makes me itch to cycle for miles!)

I've cycled since I was a little girl. Certainly cycling and roller skating were the favorite after-school pastimes of my friends from grade school and in the neighborhood. My first introduction to cycling and its fantastic connection to travel was a trip that I took at age twelve with my mother, my aunt, and uncle in France. The four of us cycled through the Loire valley. It was my first trip to France and I had a ball. I learned how to keep up with the grownups while discovering the country.

I think it's that first trip to France with family that really opened my eyes to what travel via bike could be. I found at that early age how cycling allows you to see things close up. And, that, if you want, you can easily stop to take an even closer look, stop for a chat with someone, stop for a snack, or really do whatever your heart desires.

That same aunt and uncle mentioned above are some of my closest relatives and are very precious to me. I have a small family—and these are

Figure 2

two people who have loomed large in my life. They live in London, and so I've had the benefit throughout the years of growing up visiting them in the United Kingdom and having their home as a base from which to extend many other exciting trips. As an adult my solo cycling jag really began with visiting them. I've been able to see them and take in London—one of my all-time favorite cities. I've also been able to rent a bicycle in London and cycle to all points beyond in the United Kingdom. I've started and ended cycling trips to Bulgaria and the Netherlands with visits to their home.

As of late, after taking in many western European countries, I've felt enticed to expand my travels to non-western countries, starting with Vietnam (which was incredible!), Sri Lanka, Bulgaria, and Mexico. All via bicycle (fig. 4 Hindu temple at Hawagala Mountain in Sri Lanka, 2018).

These trips stretch my brain and my understanding of the world, and allow me to connect layers of meaning of people, places, and things through time. Each trip underlines to me just how much we're all alike as humans. And at the same time I get to see just how cultures are different from each other.

I have encountered tremendous openness and friendliness traveling as a woman. I have had some really amazing experiences, particularly with other women that have buoyed me at the time, but have also inspired me to this day. Those experiences are too numerous to mention, but they include

Figure 3

meeting some fantastic Korean women in Germany and traveling together for several days and exploring the Indian Ocean with a brilliant Sri Lankan woman in Sri Lanka.

It's this sisterhood that is a part of what I love so much with travel—particularly as a solo female traveler. I've had many women—and indeed some men—encourage me in my travels, and share my delight and discovery.

That said, traveling solo—cycling solo—is not without its hitches for a woman. I have encountered much sexual harassment throughout the years—both close to home and abroad—on my bicycle, but I've remained resolved to be strong and find a way to turn any harassment or adversity into an exercise in empowerment. While admittedly difficult, I've been able to turn the negative experiences into affirmations that I am just as "allowed" and "okay" in any of the spaces that I inhabit. And these experiences have allowed me to assert that I am here and allowed to do what I love. It has given me the opportunity to stand up to the male gaze with defiance and self-reliance. I've sailed past men stopped in Bulgaria and at home openly (and lewdly: sometimes with body parts exposed) soliciting me. That feels powerful, and not only seems so on a personal level like I'm surpassing this, but I believe it is much bigger than just me.

Since cycling is a positive outlet for me, it also teaches me several practical skills. I get to learn how to navigate locations and figure out

Figure 4

Figure 5

directions and timing. And if I am traveling the sort of trip in which I don't have a preconceived idea of where I'm ending up at the end of any given day, it allows me calculating distance. I get to make my own itinerary—one that I can choose to follow or not. But it's all up to me, which is so empowering (fig. 5 bike in Iceland, 2017).

I feel strong cycling on the inside and the outside. I love the muscles that I get with my long bike rides and I admit to being a fiend about keeping track of mileage (though this is only personal competition—I'm not a competitive person at all).

The deep sense of freedom and fun that I feel every time I bike cannot be overstated. My bicycle is at once a practical vehicle (which is, in and of itself, a great thing) but it's also the means to connecting with others and ultimately—and deeply—with myself.

It is all of these things that draw me to cycling and make me feel compelled to do it. I love how the bicycle is a passport to learning about the world, other people, and myself. It's also about feeling strong and empowered. And it's about standing up for myself, self-affirmation, and self-assertion.

Traveling—wherever it is—is one of the most thrilling experiences there is. The same can be said of cycling. Put the two together and this makes for what is—in my eyes—the most dynamic way to explore, taste adventure, and learn on so many levels. It's this specific way of travel and adventure that has kept me thrilled, learning, and empowered!

Finding Our Familiars at the Lānaʻi Cat Sanctuary

Laila Brown

It's hard to find a better single word to describe the Lānaʻi Cat Sanctuary than magical. It's so unlikely that it feels unreal. Here, six hundred cats roam and luxuriate in a grassy and tree-laden three-acre haven with enough beloved sunspots for all. The sanctuary is magical because those running it work hard to make sure that the residents can enjoy the highest quality of life—including compassionate medical care, adequate space, nutritious food, and mental wellbeing—and they deserve every credit. It's magical because the sanctuary is a system motivated by a love of and deep care for animals; the employees create refuge in a way that is so rarely this comprehensive and successful. And because caring for others, including animals, is, to me, a feminist act, this place is both a literal sanctuary for what would otherwise be stray cats, and a metaphorical sanctuary free of the violence of cruelty, contempt, and apathy that cats—and women—are so often subjected to.

When three of my friends and I journeyed to the cat sanctuary, we framed our trip as a feminist pilgrimage. It was an opportunity to enact self-care by spending time in a heartwarming cat utopia, and it was a celebration of the triumph of these six hundred animals over the duplicitousness they have been associated with throughout history. For the four of us, taking a day trip together was one of the regular but perhaps under-examined ways in which we enact feminism: through inclusion of one another, and through caring for ourselves, others, and the environment.

As feminists, we foster respect for ourselves and then extend it to other women, other humans, and other animals. We see our own vitality reflected in them. Thinking this way, we feel connected to the cats. And in this place of sanctuary, we could draw a parallel between the feminist reality we seek and what the cats have achieved. It is especially satisfying because cats have been historically demonized, yet here they are respected. Their sanctuary is a manifestation of the ideals of equity and caring. In this space, we see feminist ideals aligning with feminist practice.

Women and cats are so deeply entangled in the collective consciousness that we have a word denoting both: pussy. A pussy can be either a "vagina" or a "domestic cat." To call someone (usually a man) a pussy is to insult them; to imply cowardice and weakness, to equate them with a bit of female anatomy, or more simply, with the idea of female—which, in misogynistic culture, works as an insult. When used in this way, this term is a slur, abusive to female-bodied individuals. While female-bodied individuals are taught that our anatomy repulses, male-bodied individuals learn that their anatomy carries no shame. When we use terms associated with male genitalia as descriptors—"he's a dick," or "he's so cocky"—we hear the license we give to men to be bold, brash, and uncaring. You don't have to be ashamed if you have a penis, because to have a penis is to be allowed not to care.

Being reduced to our sexual parts is commonplace for women. I'll always be awed by the mother of my friend who found a creative way to call this out. She had a male boss who, rather than look her in the eye when he was talking to her, instead chose to address her breasts. The blatant fixation with the body she lived in (and the disregard for the actual person inside the body) drove her mad. One day, as this boss proceeded to talk to her (or her chest, really), she patiently waited for him to come to a point at which her response was expected. She bent at the waist so that her head was a couple feet away from, but directly eye-level with his groin, politely made eye-contact with the crotch of his pants, and responded in kind. I like to think she made him think twice. But it will take many more callouts like this to untangle centuries-old assumptions about and traditions of disrespect towards women and female anatomy.

If someone calls you a pussy, it either means that you are being disparaged as weak and afraid, or that you are a domestic cat. It turns out that besides this term, women and cats have a lot more tying us together, according to society at large. We're dramatic yet cold, we're fickle and disdainful, we are temperamental and often physically unavailable. We are frigid—a misogynistic slur that could be used to describe a cat who doesn't want to be pet or a woman who doesn't want to have sex. In fact, the word "frigid" comes from medieval and early modern texts on witchcraft, which describe the spells witches put on men to make erections impossible.[1]

I bet all those spell-casting women had evil cat sidekicks. Yes, bad bitches and cats make a foreboding team indeed. And while this pairing has long been feared and reviled, I think the scales of popular perception are tilting away from terrifying and towards intriguing. Feminists know we have a long way to go, yet we are making progress. Cats aren't doing bad either.

Throughout history, women have been associated with cats—as witches and their feline companions, as spinstery "crazy cat ladies," and as evil villains with their feline sidekicks (think Cinderella's wicked stepmother and her subtly named cat Lucifer; the dictatorial Queen of Hearts and her slinky and confusing Cheshire Cat; and Dolores Umbridge using the Patronus Charm to conjure a Persian cat).

Other media has countered these tropes with the representation of cats as guides and helpers (Sabrina the Teenage Witch and her cat Salem; Kiki and her cat Jiji; Thackery Binx of *Hocus Pocus*). Recent representations are reframing the horror-laden conception of bloodthirsty witches into more palatable, even sometimes beloved characters. In many ways, we haven't quite moved past the association between cats and witches, but since witchcraft is in vogue right now (and Wicca is a widespread religion), that's not necessarily a bad thing.

While both women and cats have long had to deal with negative characterization of coyness, craftiness, and coldness, their union is especially despised and feared. They are linked in the popular imagination as unsavory, yet often powerful beings. Though just as the rise of social media has fostered increasing awareness of sexism and gender inequality through intersectional third and fourth wave feminism and the #MeToo movement, the proliferation of cat videos across the internet has similarly helped to reposition cats as benign, hilarious, and loveable creatures. How many hours have you spent this month watching cats be adorably nutty on YouTube? I think it is possible that because of their historical linkage, popular perceptions of women and cats have a reciprocal relationship: when one enjoys improved status and respect, so does the other.

---

1   Peter Cryle and Alison Moore, *Frigidity: An Intellectual History* (Basingstoke, U.K.: Palgrave Macmillan, 2011).

One woman who contributed in her own way to this reconceptualization of cats is Kathy Carroll, founder of the nonprofit Lānaʻi Cat Sanctuary.[2] She used her power for good: the sanctuary is home to more than six hundred cats who receive care from the kitten to kupuna (Hawaiian for "elderly") stages of life. The organization also successfully protects endangered birds by moving the cats who hunt them out of the birds' natural habitats. When a friend of mine and I discovered our mutual love and respect for cats, the realization felt serendipitous—we immediately began planning a trip to the sanctuary. We live on Oʻahu, Hawaiʻi, only a short plane ride from Lānaʻi. My friend and I were, at the time, library and information science graduate students at the University of Hawaiʻi at Mānoa, and as we discussed this upcoming trip in the communal spaces of our graduate program, many of our peers expressed interest in joining. What began as a duo happily doubled to become a group of four women making a pilgrimage to celebrate the Lānaʻi cats and the Hawaiian (and I'd argue feminist) ideal of mālama: to honor, preserve, and care for others (including animals) and the local ecosystem.

The four of us met at the Honolulu airport early one morning and boarded a terrifyingly tiny inter-island airplane. My seatmate, bafflingly, laughed like a maniac as the plane careened across the sky. After an (emotionally but realistically not that physically) turbulent flight, we landed on what I'm tempted to tritely describe as a gem in the middle of the sea. Within minutes, we were off the plane and bounding out of the one-room airport. We could, according to our phones, walk to the sanctuary in thirty minutes. On an island with the population of just over 3,000, where everyone mostly knows everyone else, we must've been a strange sight—four bright-eyed students trekking along with neither supplies nor discernible purpose. A couple people in trucks pulled over to ask us if we were okay. "We are going to visit your cat sanctuary!" So obviously, yes we were fantastic. We found a weird curved knife on the side of the road and kicked it into the grass, joking that this would be foreshadowing in a horror movie about hitchhiking. We chatted about the thesis defense and the oral exam we had just passed, the last few final projects we needed to finish before the end of the semester, and graduation. We were celebrating work we had completed,

---

2   Lānaʻi Cat Sanctuary, "Saving Cats, Protecting Birds," accessed April 14, 2019, https://lanaicatsanctuary.org/about-us/.

the kind that feels very dire before it is finished, and then as soon as it is over, releases you into the kind of ease and lightness you feel only after being relieved from great pressure. Before we knew it, we had arrived, right as the sanctuary was opening to visitors for the day.

One staff member welcomed us, as others farther off waved genially, and dragged hoses through the grass, watering the plants, and still more hefted sagging bags of cat food over their shoulders, refilling all the bowls. The sanctuary is all outdoors, a large grassy space enclosed by a wire fence. We could already see some of the cats as we approached. They were having a relaxing morning, lounging on the ground, sunbathing and licking their shiny coats. The employee brought us into the first enclosed area, which led through a door to the rest of the sanctuary. He explained that the two enclosures separate from the main enclosure were for cats with feline leukemia and cats with feline AIDS, respectively. New residents are acquired via traps set up by both the sanctuary and by the natural resources department in native bird-sensitive areas. When new cats are brought to the sanctuary, they are tested for a range of illnesses, vaccinated for the gamut of them, microchipped, spayed or neutered, and treated for any health conditions they may have. A vet flies in once a week from O'ahu to care for everyone, and those who need medication wear collars with medical information on them, so that the employees can keep everyone straight. As the employee explained this to us and we stood within the first enclosure, the cats seemed to perk up, and on their own or in groups of two or three, they came and lined up at the fence, some of them standing on their back legs, stretching up to greet us. Collectively mesmerized, we walked toward their chorus of chirrups and meows and went in.

The employee greeted each cat by name as we walked around the wide yard, under the dense canopy of trees where panther-like cats lounged across wide branches, through the central food station—a multi-level structure of wooden platforms covered in furballs in repose—and around the garden area where a couple of the feistier residents disagreed over who got to sit in an evidently coveted lounge chair. In one of the open-air structures, our guide pointed out the ladder that lead to a platform high above our heads, down from which several pairs of bright eyes peered at us. He explained that the cats up there were new residents, formerly stray cats, seventy-five percent of whom (according to the general trend) would one day feel comfortable enough to consort with human visitors after observing the many cat-human interactions of their peers that turned out to be okay.

He also gestured to the big patches of elephant grass, which concealed numerous wooden homes for the cats who preferred individual refuge. As we walked through the grounds, a handful of cats—apparently the resident ambassadors—accompanied us and our human guide, occasionally brushing up against our legs, making meaningful eye contact and mewling.

There is a "kitten garden" where all the kittens live together with ample toys and areas to be cozy. While adult cats are not allowed in the kitten garden for fear that they might bully the kittens, there is one exception—a singularly large and fluffy male who has proven to be the picture of patience and affection with the energetic teacup-sized kits, who bat at his ears and slide down his back.

One striking characteristic of the majority of the cats here is their diminutive size. They are generally about two-thirds the size of an average domestic cat. They're lithe and light, which I know because they readily stand on you as soon as you sit down anywhere. More important than their cuteness however, is that they are clearly both healthy and happy. Even the sweet elderly blind cat with a cancerous growth on her nose is rightfully treated to gentle pets and attention from her adoring caretakers.

My friends and I took the beach towels the employees offered to us, so we could stretch out on the grass ourselves among our new companions. Copying the cats and getting into relaxing positions was actually more difficult than one would think, because as soon as we threw our towels out onto the ground, two or three cats would find their way onto them, and bound by the universal rule that applies to all cats, leave barely enough room for the human. And as fun as it is to pretend to be peeved that the cats have stolen your towel, this is exactly why we came. We love these animals, we want to be surrounded by them, and we want to experience, even just briefly, an environment that supports the self-actualization of beings we adore.

People love to watch cats on the internet, and people also love to watch women on the internet, in other forms of media, and in real life. Is being in the cat sanctuary so satisfying because, for once, we are allowed to be the oglers and not the ogled? But no, I think, our gaze isn't the objectifying one so often directed at women; it's one of appreciation, of admiration.

Looking around at my three friends, each sprawled on the grass with multiple, tiny cats on their laps, the sun beaming down to vivify the green of the grass and the red of the rusted volcanic dirt, I felt balanced and healthy.

To be a feminist (to me, because there are many different *feminisms*) means to care about women and gender equality, and also to care about one another and for the environment and its myriad ecosystems. To think as a feminist can be tiring because it means being a reflexive thinker, unlearning misogyny that I've internalized, and often taking issue with interpersonal interactions and media because of their overt or quiet sexism, racism, heteronormativity. I have so much more learning to do, and there are so many things that I don't know, but one thing I am sure of is that all of this caring should not be relegated to women, or even gendered at all. It should be universally applied and upheld, as should feminism. In addition to caring for others, *doing* feminism involves caring for the self. Our trip to the sanctuary, at the end of a hectic semester, was an act of self-care. It was something that we had looked forward to for months and months, and then enjoyed immensely. A journey—even just an island hop—can be feminist with the right intention behind it.

The sanctuary charges no visitor fee and survives on donations, so we gave what our student budgets allowed, thanked the employees for their dedication to the health and happiness of the cats, hoisted our backpacks back on, and began the walk back to Lānaʻi airport and our upcoming flight home, all a little changed, I think: calmer and perhaps a bit more hopeful.

Journeying can be a feminist act, in its design and intention. For us, this trip was feminist because we went to visit and support a place in which cats—intertwined with women in history and the imagination—enjoy a utopian life. It was simultaneously self-care and care for each other and for cats. The sanctuary is a place where cats, for once, get to be humans' best friends, but they are also respected as their own entities, existing and acting in their own right. Women, likewise, should feel free to act in their own interests, without threat of being perceived as deviant and unlikeable. We should get to feel a sense of sanctuary as we move through the world. "Pussy" should be a compliment.

While hackneyed terms tying women and cats together abound, conceptions of self and worth are less forthcoming. The silver lining is we don't necessarily need this validation from the outside world: we can derive our self-worth from, well, ourselves. But it would be nice if the world were more conducive to that self-actualization. At the Lānaʻi sanctuary, we witnessed our familiars enjoying space to be their whole cat selves. Women—all genders—deserve the same.

Where Was Our History?

Cindy Rinne

And She Gathered All before Her

Entryway banner #1

I took an important journey, not very far from my Southern California home, to visit *Sexual Politics: Judy Chicago's Dinner Party in Feminist Art History*, curated by Amelia Jones at the UCLA Armand Hammer Museum in April 1996. I was forty-two. My understanding of feminism and my work as an artist were changing.

This display of women's heritage art work had been in storage since 1988. The reinstall in its hometown for the first time was performed by thirteen of those who helped create the original art. At that time, *The Dinner Party* did not have a permanent home. Now it is permanently housed in the Elizabeth A. Sackler Center for Feminist Art at the Brooklyn Museum.[1]

The Dinner Party, conceived by Judy Chicago in 1974, debuted in March 1979 at the San Francisco Museum of Modern Art. Since 1975, more than 400 women and a few men worked without pay to fulfill Chicago's dream[2] to create this monumental sculpture, which is a symbolic

---

1 Judy Chicago, 2019, https://www.judychicago.com/gallery/the-dinner-party/dp-intallations/.

2 Beverly Beyette, "Guess Who Came (Again) to 'Dinner'?" *Los Angeles Times*, April 22, 1996.

history of women's achievements and women's struggles told through thir-ty-nine china-painted plates and elaborately embroidered runners which cover an open triangular table. Each setting is devoted to a mythical or historical female and represents her accomplishments or legendary pow-ers. The three corners have crocheted vestments.[3] A "heritage floor" made of 2,300 porcelain tiles bears the names of 999 additional women chosen from various countries, periods and professions in Western Civilization.

I arrived at the Hammer on a weekday, stood behind closed doors, and then entered *The Dinner Party* alone. The sanctuary was illuminated by low light that came through the floor and under the table like an altar with place settings, and the names of women forgotten in history appeared near my feet. The place settings each had a runner, plate, silverware, and chalice, reminding me of communion. At that time, I didn't know who most of the women at the table or on the floor were. Even now, I don't recognize sever-al of the names, but I could understand this gathering as ceremony and cel-ebration. Expressing the feminine as holy.

It was a cause to express the history of women and goddesses. I worked in the needlework loft where there was linen pulled over large frames on stands for the runners which allowed us to work from all sides. We overlooked the ceramic artists in Judy's studio at what is now the 18th St. Complex. The experience brought a change of perspective regarding women's history and our past achievements. I was sad to hear that after the initial exhibition of The Dinner Party in San Francisco; it was a huge struggle to get other venues to exhibit it.

Laura Larson[4]

The Dinner Party needlework runners were labor intensive and integral to the plates. Sewing and needlework were considered "women's work" and not as fine art. When I decided to switch from being a painter to work in textiles, seeing this exhibit encouraged me. I was still an artist but using a

---

3   Jane F. Gerhard, *The Dinner Party: Judy Chicago and the Power of Popular Feminism, 1970–2007* (Athens: GA, University of Georgia Press, 2013), 142.

4   Laura Larson (artist) in discussion with the author, September 2018.

new medium. My art is time-consuming, but it doesn't seem like it is as I enjoy working with fabrics from around the world and the action of stitching them together into collages. The runners were like altar cloths using design elements from the plates. They dropped over the sides of the table to show embroidery on both sides with the name, symbols for each woman, and imagery to connect with the plate. Most of the stitcheries took over a year to complete.[5]

Judy Chicago was my teacher and mentor from 1970 to 1973. In 1974 when I was a grad student at UCLA, I visited her Santa Monica studio not long after she began working on The Dinner Party. Her studio was a huge cavernous space (it had been a factory during WW2) and it was literally buzzing with activity. A group of about 30 or 40 women were seated at large, long tables; they were all busy with projects. I remember some were working on embroidery samples. What was so impressive to me was the intense activity and devotion all those present had for Judy's project.

Nancy Youdelman[6]

Burning my bra and hating men, which I now realize are false and stereotypical views of feminism, didn't connect with me as a young woman in the early 1970s. I got married to a man I loved in 1973. Still, I was affected by unequal pay and grew up at a time when women stayed at home to raise the kids even if they wanted to work. Later I discovered feminism is not about hating men; feminism desires equality for women on many levels, including more women represented at art galleries. I saw feminist artists, along with Chicago, begin using textiles, ceramics, and other crafts to redefine what art is.

During my museum visit, if there was a security guard, I didn't notice. It was just me and *The Dinner Party*. A gathering of goddesses to share their stories with a wife/mother of young children in Southern California, my home for a little over a decade. I could sense the presence of these

---

5   Gerhard, *The Dinner Party*, 112.

6   Nancy Youdelman (artist) in discussion with the author, December 2018.

foremothers. Invited to the table, I moved in closer to see the details of the plates and runners; listen to the voices of wisdom. My inheritance. A sacred silence that screamed *I am here*. A history and religion to claim as my own. Their past; my future.

My own fiber art and poetry currently aspires to give women a voice combining textiles, myth, and symbols. Throughout history the goddess and mortal women's stories have been hidden just like the story of Hatshepsut, number eight on Wing 1 of *The Dinner Party*. Hatshepsut is the first plate to have a raised relief surface for her authority as Egypt's first female pharaoh. A divine daughter of the gods. She was a successful ruler for 20 years. Men tried to downplay her role, but she is considered the fifth king of the Eighteenth Dynasty.

Hatshepsut's porcelain plate with overglaze of enamel shows a red, blue, and gold vulva of curvy lines shaped like Egyptian hairstyles. The pink and green border on the runner draw their colors from her tomb. She is depicted in her temple at Deir el-Bahari in the Valley of the Kings with her divine birth and coronation. The blue and green roundlets on the back of the runner represent pharaonic collar and colors. The front has the initial "H" with the Egyptian symbol of the eye of justice.[7]

The Heritage Floor expressed women of the world with their names hand painted in gold to match the era of each table setting. Their past invisibility fired onto the porcelain floor; not insignificant any longer.[8] The criteria: 1) Did the woman make a significant contribution to society? 2) Did she attempt to improve conditions for women? 3) Did her life illuminate an aspect of women's experience or provide a model for the future?[9]

The idea was always to find 999 women's names for the Heritage Floor. I think in the beginning [Judy Chicago] wasn't sure if there were 999 names, [but] when I went over to UCLA to research them, there were so many resources I remember I had to make a couple of trips to my car. There were secondary source books falling out of my arms. When I got back to the studio, I had

7   "Hatshepsut," Brooklyn Museum, accessed November 30, 2019, https://www.brooklynmuseum.org/eascfa/dinner_party/place_settings/hatshepsut

8   Gerhard, *The Dinner Party*, 127.

9   Gerhard, *The Dinner Party*, 130.

to ring the doorbell with my chin, and we all had this realization that we weren't going to have to make up women's history of achievement in Western Civilization. Then the anger started to grow. Why hadn't we learned about all this in school. We paid good money. We got a college education. Where was <u>our</u> history?

Ann Isolde[10]

The 14" plates were carved, sanded, painted, and contained several layers of glaze – butterfly/vulva/shell as female form on each plate. Creating the sculptural plates meant experimentation so they didn't crack.[11] As the first plate is flat (Primordial Goddess) and the plates gain texture and height, they symbolized my journey as a feminist growing in confidence. I am a part of the new history expressed in this installation.

I continued to walk around the wings of the table. I had not seen women's art presented with a focus on the vagina in a beautiful and powerful way before. It was initially disconcerting, but important as a representation of a woman's body. The 1970s was a time of expressing art on my body in designing my own clothes. Something I am returning to now is wearable fabric sculptures as an expression of women's narratives. I paused to take in the entire room one last time as people were starting to enter.

I saw the work being created in process. It's a mess. Out of weeks of chaos this Dinner Party came together in complete beauty.

Catherine Ruane.[12]

Looking today, when I am age sixty-five, at the list of thirty-nine women, I find Emily Dickinson and muse at how I am now a poet. I often write about goddesses like Sophia and Sappho, also women on the list, and I created an

---

10   Ann Isolde (artist), telephone interview with the author, September 2018.

11   Gerhard, *The Dinner Party*, 139.

12   Catherine Ruane (artist) in discussion with the author, February 2019.

art doll for the White House Christmas tree of Sojourner Truth when Bill Clinton was President. These women of *The Dinner Party* continue to inspire and speak to me. I'm thankful for the journey I made twenty-three years ago.

My Ritual Walk

Stacy Russo

1.

I recommend starting at Bancroft Way and College Avenue. Don't begin too early if you wish to look in shops and bookstores. 10 a.m. would be perfect. If the weather is nice, find a table outside at Caffe Strada. Drink your luxurious coffee. Take in the bay breeze. Daydream.

To one side you will see the University of California, Berkeley campus. To the other, a steep climb leading to the International House and more wondrous hills above where the fog will roll in later. In other directions, you have a hill descending down, down, down through the inner parts of the city until you eventually reach the bay and then, of course, you can finally look in the direction of the magical and weathered sidewalk waiting to take you on your adventure. Welcome to my ritual walk.

2.

One of the joys of my life is that I have a ritual walk. It's a walk I have taken for nearly thirty years—at first often, then sometimes with gaps of a few years in between, but mostly as an annual pilgrimage. It leads down College Avenue at the UC Berkeley campus and travels through the Berkeley neighborhood of Elmwood and on to the wondrous community of Rockridge in Oakland. When I do this walk, I feel it is one with my body and soul. The path is alive and responsive. It lives in the world as I do. It continues through storms and calm spring days. The seasons it has experienced show in its cracks and other changes, as do my face and hands. It gives me peace to know the path is there, even when I am far away.

This small stretch, measuring just two miles, contains a universe. Cafes to die for. Three simply amazing bookstores. Cuisine from a multitude of regions and countries. A wonderful fair trade store. Shops with local art. Many people on bicycles. Many also on foot. A few on skateboards. A place with knock-out burritos and chips and salsa. An expensive gourmet vegan restaurant in addition to a vegan bakery. A breakfast joint with a delish tofu scramble. A post office. Small, large, and mid-sized grocery stores. At least one bar. One Catholic Church. A great movie theatre. Run-down apartments. Homes I love to admire that I will never be able to afford with gardens I will never be able to afford that I mistakenly thought I would be able to afford once I had my Berkeley degree. A BART station that can take you to San Francisco. Many trees, plants, trashcans, and bus stops.

Some things have come and gone over the last twenty-five or so years, but other things have remained the same. Some old things are better gone; some new things are better than what was there before; and some things are deeply missed, but it all carries on. Just like life.

3.

When I arrived at UC Berkeley in 1991 as a community college transfer student, I was slightly older than my peers. My couple of years working at various "hell jobs;" my reality as a first-generation college student; the fact that I could tell many of my classmates came from considerable wealth; and my incredibly rebellious teenage years made me feel a bit like an outsider. I placed the grit of my punk rock youth and the support I received from my parents, including lovely handwritten notes from my mom and letters my dad crafted on his old typewriter, beneath me as a sturdy foundation and continued on. That first year at Berkeley I got a job within a few days at a combined newsstand and smoke shop across the street from campus and settled in to my shared room in the student co-op housing.

While attending the community college as a full-time student, I somehow managed to get almost perfect grades, even though I continued to go to punk shows, stay out late, often drink excessively, and work full-time in a terrible job in the basement of a Sears store. I tried to continue my rebel girl lifestyle when I got to Berkeley, but thankfully the number of books I was required to read as an English major (one semester it was around forty), along with all those tough papers I had to write, made me give up drinking. I recall thinking to myself that I would never be able to do the required reading if I was drunk.

Before the start of my senior year, my healthier self moved into a tiny room in a place called The Carlton, or what my friend described as a "residential hotel." Although I didn't realize it at the time, since the stress from school, trying to sound "academic," and my imposter syndrome could overwhelm me, now that I'm a middle-aged woman who has been through some real shit storms, I can say that year allowed me to experience unique and unparalleled moments of bliss and freedom. That year would be the only time in my life since high school that I did not work and find myself under a pile of bills. Somedays I would lay on the grass to the side of Wheeler Hall with my backpack as my pillow and close my eyes beneath that California sun and feel like a millionaire.

Located at the busy, central intersection of Telegraph and Durant, my room on the fourth floor of the Carlton was small. Very small. It was perched above Blondie's Pizza with the sign "Make Pizza not War." I could walk a few blocks to famous bookstores: Moe's, Cody's, and Shakespeare and Company. Cafe Mediterranean was just down the street where my old roommate at the co-op told me Allen Ginsberg sat and wrote the footnote to *Howl*. In my room I had a card table with two metal chairs, a dresser, a sink, a microwave, a bookshelf, and a folding twin futon mattress I would put away during the day. I mostly lived on frozen bean and cheese burritos that came in a 10-pack and vegetarian Top Ramen. There was a shared bathroom down the hall.

Picked up and placed somewhere else, the room would have been drab and depressing, but here location was key and the room had one magnificent thing: a grand old window I could easily push up with my hands. From that window, the world appeared. I saw bands perform, arts and crafts vendors selling their wares, early morning trash collectors, one time a riot, many nude people, lines forming at the ATM across the street, one time a body being taken from an alley on a stretcher, political protests, bands of people dressed in costumes, and a diverse and eclectic array of human beings. Certain days when I saw bubbles floating above people's heads and even climbing up close to my window, I knew the local celebrity and poet Julia Vinograd, also known as "The Bubble Lady," must be within the crowd on the sidewalk with her wand and bubble potion in hand. Sometimes while in my magical domain, a friend looking up would see me in the window and yell up from the sidewalk, "Stacy!"

From my window, I could also look toward College Avenue two blocks up with a slight incline. I'm not sure what drew me there in that direction, but soon I found myself often walking up to College and turning in the direction away from campus. I walked and walked and walked all around Berkeley, but especially down that stretch of College Avenue into Oakland. I almost always walked alone. This walk became one of my most memorable experiences from Berkeley. In addition to quitting drinking, I also stopped smoking. In a sense, my life was becoming more harmonious. Not only was my mind expanding, but I was caring for my physical self. On these walks, I also felt a feeling of liberation that was intertwined with joy. My punk rock years had awakened me to animal rights, class inequalities, women's rights, crimes against the environment and more, and this awareness resulted in me spending many years being horribly angry, lost, and sometimes depressed, even while doing social justice work. My political activism had not weakened while at Berkeley, but something opened for me that has remained: an important and life-changing idea that one can live life as a political statement, but continue to have joy, beauty, and discovery.

This all leads to one of the best things someone ever said to me. A few years after graduation, I was talking on the phone with my friend from Berkeley and she commented on my walking. When she spoke about it, I was then living back in Southern California, but I saw myself in my mind walking down College Avenue. "I remember," she said, "how you walked so much." And then she said, "During that time, I saw you become a woman."

So that is one of the best things someone ever said to me: "During that time, I saw you become a woman." When I heard it, I knew it was true. Unlike traditional and restrictive ideas of when one crosses into womanhood, that often involve sex, marriage, or children, what my friend thought of as womanhood involved independence, motion, and self-reliance. The fact that she tied this in her mind to my solitary walks down College Avenue filled me with a deep and satisfying feeling. By this time, I was already returning to Berkeley most years to do the walk that would become my lifelong ritual.

4.

One early memory from my walk sticks with me vividly all these years later. I was on the stretch near the Rockridge area when from within a blur of people one of my professors appeared. She was rather short with wild, tangled black hair and a very large nose. "Elegantly disheveled" is a phrase that comes to mind when I recall her in my memory. During this encounter, she was holding a brown grocery bag in her arms. Various things were popping out, including a sourdough loaf. "Well, hello there!" she said to me when we came almost face to face. I was intimidated by most of my professors, including her, so this out-of-context moment was not something I could easily navigate, but I didn't need to. She was gracious.

"Are you having a good day?" she asked me. I said I was.

"Just out for a walk?" she asked.

I replied something like, "Yes, just looking around."

"Well, good then!" she told me with a confidence well beyond my years. There was a vibrancy in her face. Something like happiness. Contentment.

That was about the extent of the encounter. Such a small pocket in time, and it showed me something that I imagine now were my projections, but who really knows? What I saw in that moment was an older woman who seemed not to give a rat's ass about how she looked to others. She was thoroughly enjoying her life. It was also a glimpse into an academic woman's life. It showed me possibilities of how I could make a life with interior riches over what was on the exterior. I saw a version of success that deeply resonated. In many ways, what I saw in her that day is a form of contentment, joy, and success that I have worked to cultivate for myself.

5.

Over the decades, I have done my ritual walk in the midst of bliss, but also in moments of uncertainty and regret. I have walked it on sunny days, beneath overcast skies, and once in a delicious rainstorm where I turned up ecstatically happy, wet, and messy at a café—considerably more disheveled than my former professor. I also walked it as a statement of surviving domestic abuse. I walked it to show I was liberated. I walked it to figure things out. I walked it as a celebration of just being in the world. Only once did I walk it listening to music. Almost always, I walked it wearing my old red knit hat.

A ritual walk is one of those things that adds celebration and rhythm to our lives with little cost. A free, yet rich, gift. Some of my favorite writers and poets (Mary Oliver, Clarissa Pinkola Estés, Pablo Neruda, Thich Nhat Hanh) have taught me that one does not need a lot to live a wondrous life. Around us, if we remain awake, present, and aware, we have what I call "everyday magic"—seeing the luminosity in the commonplace and daily rituals of a lifetime.

Sometimes when I talk with students in my office and we get on the topic of living a life, I recommend they never lose the wonder and excitement for something simple they enjoy—an apple, an orange, their morning coffee, or whatever it may be. This is because you can have millions and feel as if you have nothing or you can have what others may think is not too much, but you feel wealthy. This does not mean that I do not want my students to have rewarding careers that provide good and fair wages that free them of the terrible struggles most of them face. Of course I want them to have this, but I want them to also have something like my annual pilgrimage. A magical walk.

At the time of this writing, it is early July. Summertime. I'm forty-nine. I've been invited for an author event in Berkeley. How perfect! I decided to extend my stay one day, since it's time for another walk — the last ritual walk of my forties. I leave in about two weeks.

Contributor Bios

Amanda LaTasha Armstrong earned her master's degree in child development with a specialization in administration from Erikson Institute. Currently, she is a doctoral candidate at New Mexico State University's (NMSU) Department of Curriculum and Instruction in the College of Education. Her research interests include the intersection of early childhood, learning design and technology, and issues of culture and diversity. She is also NMSU's Learning Games Lab Coordinator, where she leads user-testing sessions and teaches summer sessions focused on game design and evaluation with youth. She is a founding member of KidMap, an organization that advocates for diversity and inclusiveness in children's media, and was recently a member of the Technical Working Group to refresh the ISTE Standards for Educators. Before coming to NMSU, Amanda was the program coordinator at the TEC Center at Erikson Institute, where she supported teachers and parents in using technology and media with young children.

Laila Brown has a master's degree in Library and Information Science from the University of Hawai'i at Mānoa. She works as an academic librarian in Honolulu. Her research focuses on how participation in book clubs that espouse feminist, progressive, and diversity-oriented ethics inspire library and information science professionals to create deeper, more insightful connections between these values and librarianship. She is an advocate for equitable access to information, and she seeks to advance intersectional feminism through writing and conversation. Her small black cat, Ramona, loves to help her write by walking across her computer keyboard.

Indra Chopra is a reporter, copy editor, researcher, and writer with over twenty years of experience. She has contributed to various publications in India, the Middle East, Hong Kong, and online content. Her personal blog, travtrails.com, highlights her journeys across lands and seas. She is a guest blogger at www.tripatini.com. Indra has a Masters in English Literature from Allahabad University and a Certificate in Journalism from Stanford University.

Nina Clements earned an MFA in creative writing from Sarah Lawrence College and is the author of the poetry chapbook *Set the Table*, published by Finishing Line Press. She works as a librarian in Madison, Wisconsin.

LeeRay M. Costa is Professor and Director of Gender and Women's Studies at Hollins University. She is trained as a feminist cultural anthropologist, and her current work explores the intersection of feminist and womanist theories of social justice and embodied contemplative practice and theory in educational settings and in social justice activism. Dr. Costa seeks to nurture beloved community and to create a transformative learning environment where students feel empowered to think critically and self-reflexively, and where they are inspired to vision and create human flourishing and planetary justice. Dr. Costa is co-founder of the Hollins Contemplative Collective, which seeks to cultivate the holistic well-being of faculty, staff, and students. In 2015 she walked 400 miles on the Camino de Santiago, from Lisbon, Portugal to Santiago, Spain. Her work has appeared in the *Journal of Contemplative Inquiry*, *Feminist Teacher*, *Transformations*, and *Women's Studies Quarterly*.

Sarah Rafael García is a writer, community educator, and traveler. Since publishing *Las Niñas* (Floricanto Press 2008), she founded Barrio Writers, LibroMobile, and Crear Studio. She is an editor for the *Barrio Writers and pariahs: writing from outside the margins* anthologies. In 2016, Sarah Rafael was awarded for *SanTana's Fairy Tales* (Raspa Magazine 2017), which was supported in part by The Andy Warhol

Foundation for the Visual Arts, through a grant supporting the Artist-in-Residence initiative at California State University, Fullerton Grand Central Art Center. In 2018, she participated in a collaborative artist residency at The Guesthouse, Cork, Ireland and was honored as an Emerging Artist at the 19th Annual Orange County Arts Awards. Currently, she spends her days stacking books at LibroMobile, providing interdisciplinary literary arts workshops, and juggling time to write in Santa Ana, California.

Cass Hartnett began her career shelving fiction books at the Plattsburgh Public Library. She has been employed at the University of Michigan Library (Research Library Residency Program), the University of Michigan—School of Information, and the Detroit Public Library. She currently serves as US Documents Librarian and Gender, Women, and Sexuality Studies Librarian at the University of Washington Libraries. She also serves as affiliate faculty at the University of Washington Information School, teaching LIS 526 (Government Information). She is a cofounder of the Northwest Government Information Network (NGIN) and was 2008–2009 chair of the American Library Association's Government Documents Round Table. With colleague Kian Flynn, she co-authored "Cutting through the Fog: Government Information, Librarians, and the Forty-Fifth Presidency" for *Reference & User Services Quarterly*. She was named the University of Washington Distinguished Librarian, 2016.

Sarah L. Hastings is a Professor of Psychology and Director of Women's and Gender Studies at Radford University. Her research explores socio-cultural factors related to women's health and well-being. She has recently published a chapter exploring misogyny in American education and an essay titled "Mapping Well-Being: Reflections on the Role of Place in Healthy Human Functioning."

Wild interests and an inclination to rage against the machine with a flair that could equal the groupies and rock stars who fascinate her, **Lucretia Tye Jasmine** earned a BFA in film from NYU (University Honors Scholar), and an MFA in Critical Studies from CalArts. Veganism and feminism are primary themes as Lucretia deconstructs complicity and glamour. Alien She, MoPOP, the Museum of Broken Relationships, and the Punk Museum Los Angeles exhibited her work. The Getty Center; Duke University's Rare Book archives; and NYU's Fales Special Collections Library house some of her films and zines. An award-winning writer published in *Women Who Rock: From Bessie to Beyoncé, Grrrl Groups to Riot Grrrl,* Evelyn McDonnell, ed., (2018), and *Let It Bleed: How to Write a Rockin' Memoir,* Pamela Des Barres, ed., (2017), Lucretia's currently working on two oral history mixtape zines: *riot grrrl Los Angeles 1993–1995* and *The Groupie Gospels.*

Elizabeth Kenneday, an Emeritá Professor of Art at the California State University in Long Beach, is an artist and author. A recipient of a Fulbright Scholar Fellowship at the University of Iceland, her activities in environmental education through art have led to numerous lectures at international conferences in Europe and North America, and her writings on the subject have appeared in various publications. Her artworks have been exhibited internationally and widely collected, and she has been the recipient of many awards, most recently a Julia Margaret Cameron award in the Cell Phone photography category. Her book *Regarding Mono Lake: Novelty and Delight at an Inland Sea,* released in 2014, received an Eric Hoffer Finalist Award in Small Press Publishing in the Art category. She currently lives with her husband in Reno, Nevada.

Annie Knight is a librarian, artist, and traveler who lives in Santa Ana, California. She was born in Riverside, California, and continues to honor her Inland Empire roots. She is also a lifelong zinester and D.I.Y. advocate and is a member of the Zineworks artist collective.

Collectively, the **Lazy Bottoms** are eight female faculty from East Carolina University and one nurse at Vidant Medical Center in Greenville, NC. They represent three different colleges and seven different departments. **Anne Swenson Ticknor** is Associate Professor in the Department of Literacy Studies, English Education, and History Education. **Paige Averett** is Professor and Director of Graduate Programs in the School of Social Work. **Allison Crowe** is Associate Professor and Program Coordinator in the ECU Counselor Education Program. **Anna Froula** is Associate Professor of Film Studies in the

Department of English. **Cindy Grace-McCaskey** is Assistant Professor in the Department of Anthropology. **Jennifer F. McKinnon** is Associate Professor and Director of Graduate Studies in the Department of History Program in Maritime Studies. **Stacy L. Weiss** is Associate Professor of Special Education. **Amanda Klein** is Associate Professor of Film Studies in the English Department at East Carolina University. **Amber Wigent** is a Critical Care Registered Nurse.

Valeria E. Molteni has a Licensure in Librarianship and Documentation from the National University of Mar del Plata, Argentina; a Master of Science in Information Studies from the University of Texas at Austin; and PhD coursework from the University of Granada, Spain. She has worked as an academic and special librarian in Argentina and the USA. Valeria worked at the Benson Collection at University of Texas in Austin; as the Multicultural and Outreach Librarian at California State University, Dominguez Hills; and as Academic Liaison Librarian and interim Associate Dean for Research and Scholarship at the MLK Library, San José State University. Currently she is the Dean of Library Services at Menlo College, Atherton, California. She has published journal articles, book chapters, and conference presentations on the analysis of scientific production; on the evaluation of university research systems; on electronic journal collections; on library instruction and services for international and bilingual populations; and on spaces in academic libraries.

Leah Jane Oliver is a dancer-poet-librarian living in Upstate NY.

Anya Ravitz is a National Certified Counselor (NCC) and mental health counselor working in a methadone clinic. She is committed to helping others discover their self-worth and developing a strong sense of identity. Her writing can be found in *Body Love 4 All Global Zine: Our Journey to Body Love*, *On the Margins*, *The Architect's Newsletter*, and *ArchitectureWeek*. She lives in Chicago with her wonderful partner, Mike, and their two cats, Molly and Tabitha.

Jana Remy is the Director of Educational Technology at Chapman University and holds a Ph.D. in History from the University of California, Irvine. She teaches courses in Disability History and Digital

Humanities. In her free time she grows organic veggies, posts food pictures to Instagram, and paddles outrigger canoes on the ocean. She lives in Santa Ana, California, with Stijn, EllyCat, and Maru-MaruMoMo-san.

Cindy Rinne creates art and writes in San Bernardino, California. She gathers world stories and brings myth to life in contemporary context. Cindy is the author of seven books: *Mapless* with Nikia Chaney (Cholla Needles Press), *Moon of Many Petals* (Cholla Needles Press), *Listen to the Codex* (Yak Press), *Breathe In Daisy, Breathe Out Stones* (FutureCycle Press), and others. She is a founding member of PoetrIE, a literary community and a finalist for the 2016 Hillary Gravendyk Prize. Her poetry appeared or is forthcoming in: *Birds Piled Loosely, Home Planet News, Outlook Springs, The Wild Word* (Berlin), *Storyscape Journal, Event Horizon Magazine, Anti-Herion Chic, Mojave River Review*, several anthologies, and others. Visit her website at www.fiberverse.com.

Stacy Russo, a librarian and associate professor at Santa Ana College in Santa Ana, California, is a writer, poet, and artist who is committed to creating books and art for a more peaceful world. Her book publications include *A Better World Starts Here: Activists and Their Work* (Sanctuary Publishers); *Love Activism* (Litwin Books); *We Were Going to Change the World: Interviews with Women from the 1970s and 1980s Southern California Punk Rock Scene* (Santa Monica Press); *Life As Activism: June Jordan's Writings from The Progressive* (Litwin Books); *The Library as Place in California* (McFarland); and two poetry chapbooks: *The Moon and Other Poems* (Dancing Girl Press) and *Everyday Magic* (Finishing Line Press). Stacy's books have been featured on National Public Radio, Pacifica Radio, the Canadian Broadcasting System, Sirius XM Radio, KCET Artbound, LA Weekly, and various other media channels. Her articles, poetry, and reviews have appeared in *Feminist Teacher, Feminist Collections, American Libraries, Counterpoise, Library Journal, Chaffey Review, Serials Review*, and the anthology *Open Doors: An Invitation to Poetry* (Chaparral Canyon Press). Stacy is a collage artist. She uses magazines, old books, acrylic paint, cardboard, and wood in her creations.

She holds degrees from the University of California, Berkeley; Chapman University; and San Jose State University.

Alison Stankrauff is the University Archivist at Wayne State University. She has a Masters in Library and Information Science with a Concentration on Archival Administration from Wayne State University (2002). She has a Bachelors in History from Antioch College (1996). She has been at Wayne State since September 2017. Previous to that she was the University Archivist and an Associate Librarian at Indiana University South Bend from 2004 to August 2017. Prior to that she served as Reference Archivist at American Jewish Archives from 2002 to 2004.

Jie Tian is a poet, librarian, ecological artist, and holds an MFA in Creative Writing from the University of California, Riverside. She has received residency awards from Hedgebrook and Djerassi Resident Artists Program. Her poems, essays, and reviews appeared in *Pearl, Spillway, Squaw Valley Review, Solo Novo, Sentence: A Journal of Prose Poetics, Asian American Short Story Writers*, and *Asian American Playwrights*. She is working on a multimedia poetry project on migration that employs print, digital, and book arts tradition. This project marks a healing journey for Jie in the practice of ecological arts, including growing plant materials for natural dye, papermaking, and book making.

Trysh Travis is an Associate Professor in the Center for Gender, Sexualities, and Women's Studies Research, University of Florida, where she teaches courses in gender and popular culture, the history of Anglo American feminism, and the gendered history of medicine. She is the author of *The Language of the Heart: The Recovery Movement from Alcoholics Anonymous to Oprah Winfrey* (UNC, 2009) and co-editor (with Timothy Aubry) of *Rethinking Therapeutic Culture* (Chicago, 2016). She is also the co-founder of and a frequent contributor to *Points: The Blog of the Alcohol and Drug History Society*. Her non-academic work can be found in *Raritan: A Quarterly Review, The American Historian, Inside Higher Ed*, and *The Chronicle of Higher Education*, among other venues.

Holiday Vega is a graduate student in library and information science at the University of Hawaiʻi at Mānoa. She is conducting her thesis research on public libraries and homelessness and the partnerships between libraries and social services. She is also completing a research study on LGBTQ-targeted harassment in online video game streaming communities. She earned a Masters in Social Work from Tulane University in New Orleans, and specialized in trauma-informed care for victims and survivors of sex trafficking and commercial sexual exploitation. Her research interests are in social justice in librarianship, virtual communities and mental health, readers' response theory as applied to other forms of media, and feminist gamer culture.

Lise Weil is an award-winning editor and translator. Her memoir *In Search of Pure Lust* (2018 Inanna Publications, Canada, She Writes Press, U.S.) is a finalist for a Foreword Indies award and winner of a bronze IPPY award. She was founder of the feminist review *Trivia: A Journal of Ideas* (1982–1991) and its online offshoot *Trivia: Voices of Feminism* (2003–1011). She is currently editor of the ecofeminist journal *Dark Matter: Women Witnessing* and teaches in the Goddard College Graduate Institute. Born in Chicago, she moved to Montreal in 1990.

D. D. Wood started her writing career as a singer-songwriter for Walt Disney's Hollywood Records, where her songs were used in various Disney films. She received rave reviews for her solo albums *Tuesdays are Forever* and *Songs for the Red King*, and has played with many well-respected artists, including Chris Isaak, Willie Nelson, Emmylou Harris, Leon Russell and Rosanne Cash. D. D. currently teaches 11th grade Honors and AP English in the Compass Music and Arts program in Long Beach, California, and is actively involved in mentoring students gifted in the arts. She has a Master's degree in Education, and has achieved National Board Certification in Young Adult English. She is also an Adjunct Professor for Concordia University's MAED program. D.D. began writing her first YA novel, *The Year I Lost You*, through a fellowship to the Vermont Writer's Studio and has now completed her second novel, *Punk Rock Princess*, and is currently working on her book of humorous essays, *Saturday Stories*.

Original Call for Proposals

The original call for proposals below was posted on women and gender studies listservs, the editor's website, and the editor's personal and community social media pages.

Call for Proposals

Personal essay contributions are desired for a proposed edited book: *Feminist Pilgrimage: Journeys of Discovery.*

How is "Feminist Pilgrimage" Being Defined?

Within this context, a feminist pilgrimage is understood as one of the following:

- a journey taken to visit an important feminist landmark, artwork, or individual.

- traveling to a destination as a means of radical self-care, discovery, and/or healing, such as returning to one's home land; taking a solo road trip; going on a personal or group retreat; or making a journey to a place that has deep personal meaning.

- a pilgrimage taken for personal or professional reasons that is performed with a feminist vision.

How is Feminism Being Defined?

There are many definitions and understandings of feminism. One's understanding may also evolve over time through personal and collective experiences. For the purposes of allowing for the most self-expression and freedom in the creative process, the editor is not providing an overarching definition.

Guidelines

All genders are welcome as contributors. Only non-fiction, first-person accounts are desired. Writing should be in the form of a personal essay. Text-only works and works including artwork with text will be considered. Fictional pieces and poetry will not be accepted. Original works that have not been previously published are preferred. Previously published essays will be considered, but you will need to gain permissions for re-publication and provide proof of the permission. Writing should be free of highly theoretical language and academic jargon. Footnotes and references, if any, should be minor. Tone should be for a crossover general and academic audience.

Proposals

Please submit proposals of up to 500 words by November 1, 2018. Include an author's bio of up to 150 words. Within your proposal, please provide a clear representation of what your essay will entail. What was your pilgrimage? Where did you travel? What did you discover? Why was the pilgrimage important to you? How does it relate to your understanding of feminism? After review of your proposal, you will be contacted regarding your submission.

With Gratitude

Much heartfelt thanks to all the contributors for digging dip, being courageous, and sharing your wonderful stories. Thank you for working with me, the time spent going back and forth, and trusting me with your words. Much love and gratitude to my partner Steven Soto for his support of my work all these years. Love 24/7 to Joni for her companionship. Thank you to Dawn Finley for reading my essay and being the editor's editor. Thank you to the following people for their continued support and encouragement: Ruth King, Victoria Schlicht, Laura Beth Bachman, Angelica Figueroa Salas Head, Kate Jessica Raphael, Julie Artman, Luis Pedroza, Gustavo Hernandez, Hilary Fielding, Elise Bernal, and Dyana Valentine. Thank you to my spirit family: mom, dad, and David. Missing you here on Earth.

Stacy Russo

CPSIA information can be obtained
at www.ICGtesting.com
Printed in the USA
LVHW050212011020
667470LV00009B/23

9 781634 001113